AA

D0306642

The
Peak District

AA Publishing

Author: Tony Hopkins
Page layout: Stuart Perry

Produced by AA Publishing

First edition published 1996.
Reprinted 1996, 1998.
Second edition 1999.
Reprinted 2000.
Third edition 2002.
Reprinted 2004, 2005.

Published by AA Publishing
(a trading name of Automobile
Association Developments
Limited, whose registered office is
Southwood East, Apollo Rise,
Farnborough, Hampshire, GU14
0JW. Registered Number 1878835).

Ordnance Survey® This product
includes
mapping data licensed from
Ordnance Survey® with the
permission of the Controller of Her
Majesty's Stationery Office.
© Crown copyright 2005. All rights
reserved. Licence number 399221.

Mapping produced by the
Cartographic Department of The
Automobile Association. A02460.

ISBN-10: 0-7495-3298-X
ISBN-13: 978-0-7495-3298-7

A CIP catalogue record for this
book is available from the
British Library.

Gazetteer map references are taken
from the National Grid and can be
used in conjunction with
Ordnance Survey maps and atlases.
Places featured in this guide will
not necessarily be found on the
maps at the back of the book.

All the walks are on rights of way,
permissive paths or on routes
where de facto access for walkers is
accepted. On routes which are not
on legal rights of way, but where
access for walkers is allowed by
local agreements, no implication
of a right of way is intended.

The contents of this book are
believed correct at the time of
printing. Nevertheless, the
publishers cannot accept
responsibility for errors or
omissions, or for changes in details
given in this guide or for the
consequences of any reliance on
the information it provides. We
have tried to ensure accuracy in
this book, but things do change
and we would be grateful if readers
would advise us of any inaccuracies
they may encounter. This does not
affect your statutory rights.

Visit the AA Publishing website at
www.theAA.com/bookshop

Colour reproduction by L C Repro
Printed and bound by G. Canale &
C. S.p.A., Torino, Italy

Contents

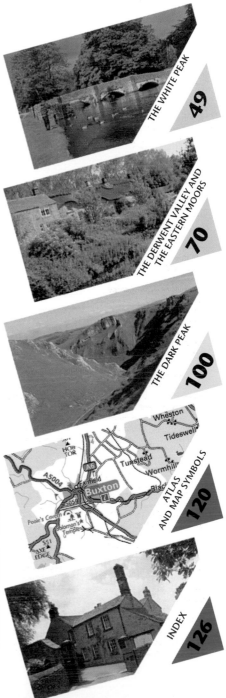

LOCATION MAP **4**

INTRODUCING THE PEAK DISTRICT **6**

A WEEKEND IN THE PEAK DISTRICT **8**

THE SOUTHERN DALES **12**

BUXTON AND THE WESTERN MOORS **30**

THE WHITE PEAK **49**

THE DERWENT VALLEY AND THE EASTERN MOORS **70**

THE DARK PEAK **100**

ATLAS AND MAP SYMBOLS **120**

INDEX **126**

WES

0 — 20 km
0 — 10 miles

Rochdale

Bury

Bolton

GREATER MANCHESTER

Oldham

Ashton-under-Lyne

MANCHESTER

Stockport

Knutsford

CHESHIRE

Middlewich

Congleton

Crewe

10

Holmfirth

Dunford Bridge

THE DARK PEA

Tintwistle

9

Glossop

High Peak

Hayfield

Edale

Ho

New Mills

Peak District

Bradwell

Whaley Bridge

Chapel-en-le Frith

Peak Fores

Bollington

Dove Holes

Macclesfield

2

1

Buxton

4

Tides

Taddin

BUXTON AND THE WESTERN MOORS

THE WH

Allgreave

Flash

Danebridge

River Dove

Monyash

3

Longnor

Harting

Upper Hulme

Warslow

THE SOUTHER DALES

Leek

Wetton

Onecote

1

Parwi

Waterhouses

Tissing

Ilam

Swinscoe

Ashbour

Stoke-on-Trent

Newcastle-under-Lyme

STAFFORDSHIRE

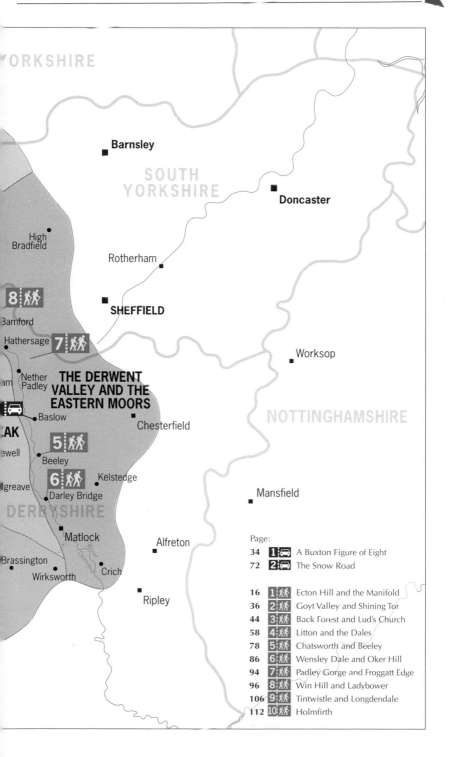

YORKSHIRE

Barnsley

SOUTH
YORKSHIRE

Doncaster

High
Bradfield

Rotherham

8

Bamford

Hathersage 7

Worksop

Nether
Padley

**THE DERWENT
VALLEY AND THE
EASTERN MOORS**

Baslow

Chesterfield

NOTTINGHAMSHIRE

AK

5

ewell

Beeley

6 Kelstedge

greave Darley Bridge

Mansfield

DERBYSHIRE

Matlock

Alfreton

Brassington

Wirksworth

Crich

Ripley

Page:

| 34 | 1 | A Buxton Figure of Eight |
| 72 | 2 | The Snow Road |

16	1	Ecton Hill and the Manifold
36	2	Goyt Valley and Shining Tor
44	3	Back Forest and Lud's Church
58	4	Litton and the Dales
78	5	Chatsworth and Beeley
86	6	Wensley Dale and Oker Hill
94	7	Padley Gorge and Froggatt Edge
96	8	Win Hill and Ladybower
106	9	Tintwistle and Longdendale
112	10	Holmfirth

Introducing The Peak District

The Peak District was England's first National Park, reflecting its importance as a landscape of rare drama and beauty. Towns and cities crept as close as they dared to the uncompromising uplands; industry has ebbed and flowed from the valleys, leaving a flotsam of millstones, lead mines and weavers' cottages. Farming has shaped the open moors and walled pastures, and been shaped in turn by climate and soil. Sandstone counterpoints limestone; high gritstone edges of the Dark Peak overlook wooded dales and the flower-studded pastures of the White Peak plateau. In no other part of England is there such diversity, touched but unspoilt by old industries, busy with visitors yet full of open space.

The landscape has inspired some of the finest writers on rural north-country life (DH Lawrence, George Eliot, Charlotte Brontë, Izaak Walton), and diverted some of the most celebrated travellers (Boswell, Defoe, Byron). Norman kings have hunted its forests, Manchester wage-slaves have hiked its byways and climbed its crags.

BAKEWELL PUDDINGS
Left, call it a Bakewell Tart at your peril – hereabouts they're definitely puddings, and very tasty, too!

BLUE JOHN
Above, Blue John, a rare and colourful fluorspar, is found only in the caverns of the Peak

CRADLE OF INDUSTRY
The Industrial Revolution took hold in Cromford in 1771 when Richard Arkwright built the world's first mechanised textile factory

MILLSTONES
Huge millstones were once quarried in the hills around Hathersage, above

LAST OF THE SUMMER WINE
Discreet traces of Nora Batty and friends are to be found in Holmfirth

ARBOR LOW
Right, Arbor Low Stone Circle, near Youlgreave, is one of the Peak District's most important prehistoric sites

10 BEST DALES AND VALLEYS
Beresford Dale
Monsal Dale
Miller's Dale
Cressbrook Dale
Dovedale
Lathkill Dale
Edale
Manifold Valley
Dane Valley
Goyt Valley

WELL-DRESSING
Well-dressing, right, is a colourful speciality of the region, in a tradition dating back for generations

BIRDWATCHING
Above, forestry and water storage have brought new uses for land, and provide a different habitat for wildlife

AN ORCHID ON THE MONSAL TRAIL
Wild flowers, such as this common spotted orchid, can be seen along Peaks footpaths

GARLAND DAY
Above, at Castleton's cheerful Garland festivities in May, a 'king' wearing a vast cone of flowers, leads the procession

ROCKY CRAGS FOR CLIMBERS
The crags of the Peak District have taken strange names, such as Hen Cloud and Mock Beggar's Hall, and many are popular with climbers

If you have little time and want to sample the essence of the Peak District... **Walk** along the top of Froggat Edge an hour before sunset... **Collect** bilberries on the slopes of The Roaches... **Send** a saucy postcard from Holmfirth (where they were invented)... **Scramble** around Mock Beggar's Hall (a gritstone outcrop near Birchover)... **Walk** around the stones of Arbor Low on a misty morning... **Hear** 'Blue-eyed Stranger', the finest of all Morris tunes, played in its home village during Winster Wakes... **Stand** on the top of Win Hill on a sunny day and see if it's raining on Lose Hill... **Look** for frogs along the Cromford Canal... **Listen** to songbirds in the oak woods of Padley Gorge... **Watch** for a ripple in Izaak Walton's Pike Pool in Beresford Dale... **Buy** a Bakewell Pudding in Bakewell and go for a picnic along the Monsal Trail.

PEAK CHEESES
Below, there are many varieties of that old favourite, Stilton, among local cheeses

KEEP RIGHT ON TO THE END
The start of the tough 256-mile (412-km) Pennine Way National Trail at Edale

A Weekend in the Peak District: Day One

For many people a weekend break or a long weekend is a popular way of spending their leisure time. These four pages offer a loosely planned itinerary designed to ensure that you make the most of your time and see and enjoy the very best the area has to offer. Options for wet weather and children are given where possible. Places with gazetteer entries are in **bold**.

Friday Night

If you can afford it, stay at Fischer's Hotel, just north of **Baslow** village on the A623 above the River Derwent. The food is superb: herbs out of the kitchen garden and venison and lamb from the nearby Chatsworth Estate. In the evening go for a short drive and stroll on to Curbar Edge, for a view of the setting sun over the White Peak.

Saturday Morning

Just up the A619 is the entrance to **Chatsworth Park**. Spend the morning walking around the magnificent house and grounds, or explore East Moor and Beeley Moor. Excellent heather moorland, with Bronze-Age settlements and barrows.

Leave Chatsworth on the A623, driving northwest up Middleton Dale, past Lovers' Leap and an octagonal toll house.

Left, go for a relaxing stroll along Curbar Edge

Below and bottom, enjoy the many delights of Chatsworth, or take to the hills around Beeley

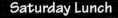
Right and below, explore hidden corners of Tideswell, and admire the splendours of the 'Cathedral of the Peak'

Saturday Lunch

Stop at the Three Stags Head at Wardlow Mires; a little stone-floored pub, serving well-kept beers from independent Sheffield breweries. Good food too, served on plates and dishes from the adjacent pottery – so you can buy what you eat off.

Saturday Afternoon

Head for **Tideswell**, either by driving further along the A623 and turning off left, or by a side-road through the pretty village of Litton. Walk round the fine parish church at Tideswell ('Cathedral of the Peak') then take the car down to the Tideswell Dale car park and walk along **Miller's Dale** as far as Water-cum-Jolly Dale, with ash trees, limestone crags and the tinkling waters of the Wye.

Right, walk through pretty Miller's Dale

Below, discover the mysterious stone circle of Arbor Low

Drive southwest on the B6049 and A5270 to meet the A515, then go southeast through Parsley Hay. At the side road for **Youlgreave**, detour for a look at the great stone circle of Arbor Low and the nearby barrow of Gib Hill; both date back to the Bronze Age. Continue on the A515 and turn right to **Hartington.**

Saturday Night

Stay at Biggin Hall, a mile to the southeast of Hartington; it comprises a cluster of 17th-century buildings with mullioned windows and oak beams. Try to book the Master Suite, complete with four-poster bed. Traditional farmhouse cooking.

A Weekend in the Peak District: Day Two

You are in the heart of the White Peak, close to the southern dales. Your second day explores this area then heads north for a tour of the Dark Peak, with alternative options depending on personal taste and the weather.

Sunday Morning

Go for an early walk down Biggin Dale, or linger over breakfast and then look round **Hartington**; feed the ducks on the pond and buy some local Stilton to take home. Then follow in the footsteps of the 'Compleat Anglers', Izaak Walton and Charles Cotton, down Beresford Dale on the quiet upper reaches of the River Dove. You can walk as far as you wish, into Wolfscote Dale and to Mill Dale, but for this you will need a packed lunch.

Further south still is famous Dovedale. If you wish you can drive to **Ilam** and take the easy short walk by the Stepping Stones to Mill Dale. But remember this route may be popular on a fine Sunday morning.

Sunday Lunch

From Hartington or Ilam head for Warslow, where you can call for lunch at the Greyhound. Wardlow is close to the Manifold Valley; a short detour down into Ecton will give you a flavour of the scenery.

Left, tour around Hartington at your leisure

Below, don't miss scenic Dovedale

Left, look out for Thor's Cave in the Manifold Valley

Right, pass through Longnor, with its grand former market hall

Below, enjoy the dramatic landscape of Winnats Pass

Right, visit the church at Chapel-en-le-Frith, with its odd dedication

Sunday Afternoon

Drive north on the road to **Longnor,** then on to **Buxton.**

There are now three options. If the weather is really unkind you can spend the afternoon here, breezing around the Pavilion Gardens.

Alternatively, head north on the A6 through Dove Holes and east on the A623 and B6061 via the dramatic Winnats Pass road towards **Castleton.** Here there are caves and Blue John mines, the oldest castle in the Peaks and some good pubs and cafés.

If you are feeling adventurous and there is no risk of blizzards (!) stay on the A6, north of Dove Holes to **Chapel-en-le-Frith,** then on to **Glossop** and turn east on the A57, crossing the **Snake Pass** and dropping down the Woodlands Valley to the **Derwent Dams**. Whichever way you go, finish at Padley, close to where you started, in the shade of sessile oaks and with pied flycatchers singing among the branches.

The Southern Dales

Middle England meets the North as you walk or drive uphill from Ashbourne Market Place. The arc of countryside from Leek through Ashbourne to Belper pays its dues to the Trent; it rolls and dips southwards to the river plain, and its tributary, the Dove, meanders gracefully through green fields and hedgerows. But on the far side of Ashbourne everything changes as the land rises and the Dove spreads out a thousand fingers into every crevice of the hills. Brooks and rivulets reach into the limestone at the Peak's core. Villages lie on the thousand-foot contour on the plateau because the valleys are so narrow; ancient ash woods clothe the slopes, dairy cattle graze the pastures, drystone walls cobweb the meadows.

THE LONGEST INN SIGN

One of the clearest images of Ashbourne for those travelling through by car is the gallows-style inn sign which spans St John's Street. Claimed as the longest inn sign in the world, it was erected when the Green Man was amalgamated with the Blackamoor in 1825. The sign proclaims 'Green Man and Black's Head', but the latter has long since ceased to function as a hostelry. The Green Man was a famous coaching inn, praised by James Boswell in 1777 and visited by Princess Victoria in 1832.

The pleasant old market town of Ashbourne has taken on the more recent tourist mantle of gateway to 'Izaak Walton Country'

ASHBOURNE Derbyshire Map ref SK1746

The old market town of Ashbourne lies in a cleft in the rolling farmland of southwest Derbyshire, a landscape of fields and hedges rather than moors and walls. Along the cleft runs the Henmore Brook on its way to meet the River Dove.

The drive into and through Ashbourne is not straightforward; there is a one-way system and the roads are often congested, but there are points on the sweep down into the town where the shape of the settlement can be appreciated. The most immediate impression is that the parish church, with its distinctive needle-sharp spire, lies some way from the town centre. This means that when you have parked there is a walk of several hundred yards if you want to take a close look at famous St Oswald's, but by doing so, and exploring the Market Place on the way, you see the very best of the town.

Ashbourne Market Place, opposite the Town Hall, used to be lined with alehouses and had its own bullring (close to the Wright Memorial, an elaborate piece of Victoriana). It was here that Bonnie Prince Charlie proclaimed his father King of England, and it was from here that the famous Shrovetide Football, between the 'Uppards' and 'Downards' of the town, always started (it was moved to Shaw Croft to reduce damage to property, but still rages along the Henmore, between the goals of Sturton Mill and Clifton Mill, each Easter). At the back of the Market Place is the Old Vaults pub, which used to be called The Anatomical Horse, with a skeleton for its sign. Down the narrow alley to the left is Victoria Square (once The Butchery and The Shambles) and Tiger Yard, beside a restaurant which used to be The Tiger Inn. The modern Victoria Square is a smart little sun-trap, set about with benches.

Ashbourne's side streets and alleys are narrow and interesting; the layout of the old town north of the Henmore dates back to the 11th and 12th centuries and there are some fascinating nooks and crannies, such as Lovatt's Yard and the House of Confinement (ie lock-up) on Bellevue Street. However, it is along St John's Street and Church Street that the town's grandest buildings are to be found. Beyond the Clergy's Widows Almshouses are mansions and merchants' houses, several now serving as antiques shops, culminating in the magnificent stone-gabled Grammar School, founded by Elizabeth I in 1585. And opposite, set back behind tall wrought-iron gates and a carpet of daffodils in the spring, stands St Oswald's Church, described by George Eliot as 'the finest mere parish church in England'.

'OAKBOURNE'
Ashbourne is a perfect example of an English market town – eccentric street plan, narrow cobbled alleys, coaching inns, almshouses and market stalls. It needed very little alteration to become the 'Oakbourne' of George Eliot's *Adam Bede*, and is probably the best place in the Peak District to explore for antiques (but don't expect many bargains!).

Topped by a grinning black head and dangling a more traditional sign, the gallows-style inn sign stretches across St John's Street

The reservoir at Carsington is a well-established local amenity

THE RUDDY DUCK

One of Carsington Water's controversial residents is the American ruddy duck. Fifty years ago this little duck (big blue bill, white cheeks, reddish back, stiff tail) was unknown outside the Wildfowl Trust, but it escaped and is now so widespread that it is threatening to over-run Europe, diluting the genes of its close relative the European white-headed duck in the process.

CARSINGTON WATER Derbyshire Map ref SK2552

New reservoirs usually take years to blend with a landscape, and sometimes they never do. Carsington, opened by Her Majesty the Queen in 1992, already looks at home in the gently rolling hills southwest of Wirksworth.

Most of the Peak District's many reservoirs gather their water off acid moorland, so they are low in nutrients, and this in turn means they are surprisingly poor for aquatic plants and animals. Carsington is quite different and shows every sign of becoming a mecca for birds and other wildlife. In the winter there are wildfowl by the thousand, including widgeon, pochard and tufted duck; in the summer there are dabchick and great crested grebes; and in the spring and autumn, at migration time, there are all sorts of unusual waders and seabirds, using the reservoir as an oasis on their way from coast to coast.

A third of the Carsington shore is set aside as a conservation area, but the rest is accessible, not only by footpath but by bicycle and by horse. The main Visitor Centre is on the west shore, with an extensive car park (for which there is a charge) off the B5035.

There are several interesting mining villages to the north of Carsington Water, including Brassington, which boasts some fine 18th-century houses and a Norman church. Inside the church, look for the even older carving high on the west wall of the tower; a naked man with his hands on his heart.

Hopton village is now dominated by the reservoir, though there is a bypass for the main road. Until 1989 Hopton Hall (not open) was the home of the Gell family, who made their fortune from the nearby limestone quarries, and made their name as scholars, politicians and travellers. Across the limestone rise to the north runs the Hopton Incline, once the steepest gradient for any railway line in Britain, using fixed engines and cable-haulage to set the High Peak Railway on its journey from Cromford Wharf to Whaley Bridge. It is now a cycle/walking route called the High Peak Trail. Further north again is the Via Gellia, a road created and named by one of the Gells, through superb flower-rich woodland along a valley west of Cromford.

NATURE RETURNED
North of Carsington and Hopton the land rises to the 1,000-foot contour, topped by a block of stone called King's Chair. This area is pock-marked by old lead mines and limestone quarries, but wild flowers abound on the open limestone and into the Via Gellia; there are places where several kinds of orchids jostle for space, and in the shade of ash woodland there are patches of the rare herb paris.

Much of the lake shore is a designated conservation area, attracting wildlife

Ecton Hill and the Manifold

The Manifold is one of the most beautiful of all the limestone dales, less visited than the nearby Dove, full of secrets waiting to be told. The walk ranges over windswept, sun-drenched grassland hills to the deep shadows of the valley, its ash woods and caves.

Time: 4 hours. Distance: 7 miles (11.3km).
Location: 9 miles (14.5km) northwest of Ashbourne.
Start: Take the A515 north from Ashbourne, after about 5 miles (8km) turn left on to a minor road and drive through Alstonefield to Wetton. Park in the Peak National Park car park on the southern edge of Wetton. (OS Grid ref: SK109552.)
OS Map: Outdoor Leisure 24
(The Peak District – White Peak) 1:25,000.
See Key to Walks on page 121.

ROUTE DIRECTIONS

From the car park turn left and left again into Wetton. At a junction follow the sign 'Manifold Valley'; when the road turns left take the footpath signed 'Back of Ecton'. Continue through a gate and squeeze stiles to a sign '**Wetton Hill**'. Continue ahead, descend to a stile and cross a field diagonally to another stile in the corner of a wall. Continue downhill with a wall on the left.

When the wall swings left keep ahead across the fields to the right of a row of hedgerow trees. Go straight up the next field and cross a stile into a walled lane. Turn left to a house, go through a gate then turn sharp right up a tarmac drive and take the left fork uphill.

Before the summit turn right through a gate and follow a wall on the left past the ruins of the old **copper mine**. Continue ahead, leaving the wall on the left, and follow the contour below the triangulation column of Ecton Hill, through old walled enclosures and go through a squeeze stile.

Go downhill with an old wall on the right. Ignore a stile ahead when the wall turns left and bear left on to a zigzag green track which leads down through old mine workings. Cross a stile, go through an archway at a folly and continue down the drive to a road. Turn left along the **Manifold Trail**.

The track hugs the Manifold for almost a mile (1.6km) until it reaches a tunnel and a road. Go through the tunnel (stay alert) and continue for just over a mile (2km) to **Wettonmill** – now a café. Beyond the mill fork left keeping close to the river and then cross it at a bridge. At the next bridge, cross back to the right bank; the trail now ceases to be a road. As the river bends left **Thor's Cave** can be seen ahead. Turn left off the main valley and cross the footbridge. Continue through the woods.

To visit Thor's Cave turn right at a signpost. Take care at the cave entrance, which can be slippery. Retrace your steps and continue through the woods and fields up a shallow valley. Go through a squeeze stile on the left, near the top corner of the last field, into a lane. Turn right and then right again into the village, then left at the next junction to return to the car park at the start of the walk.

POINTS OF INTEREST

Wetton Hill and Sugarloaf
Dry, close-cropped grassland covers the high rolling hills. The pale grey limestone was laid down 280 million years ago as a series of coral reefs in a shallow tropical sea. Cattle graze the pastures.

Ecton Copper Mines
Hidden shafts, spoil heaps and debris litter the landscape above Ecton. In the 17th and 18th centuries this was one of the biggest copper mines in Europe,

Cattle enjoy the lush pasture on Ecton Hill

with a main shaft descending to 1,400 feet (426.7m) below the Manifold.

The Manifold Trail and the Swainsley Tunnel

The Manifold Trail makes use of the old narrow-gauge line of the Leek and Manifold Valley Light Railway. The line was opened in 1904 to link up with the North Staffordshire Railway and it was hoped that movements of farm produce and lead would keep the branch busy, but the line closed after only 30 years.

Wettonmill

This old watermill, which once ground corn for the local farming community, now serves as a café. At this point the River Manifold usually disappears underground, breaking surface again 4 miles (6.4km) away at Ilam.

Thor's Cave

This is just one of an important series of caves along the upper slopes of the valley. Many have yielded secret hoards, from Saxon gold to hyena bones. Named after the Norse god of thunder, Thor's Cave is certainly the most dramatic to look at and to view from. It is said that the silence of the shadows is disturbed now and then by the ghost of a demented fiddler.

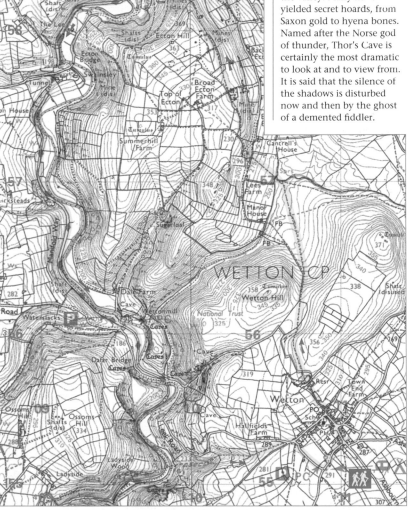

The uneven spans of Viator Bridge mark the division of Dovedale and Mill Dale

THE SPREADING SYCAMORES
Trees can be a curse as well as a blessing. Sycamores were virtually absent from Dovedale until the end of the 18th century, and Victorian tourists would have seen the famous rock formations, such as the Twelve Apostles and Pickering Tor, framed in a scatter of ash rather than buried in a sea of sycamore. These days the National Trust keeps the invasive sycamore in check, whilst encouraging the native ash. But on the windswept uplands it is a different story; sycamore still makes the best shelter belts and would be sorely missed.

DOVEDALE Derbyshire/Staffordshire
Fame, beauty and availability are a heady mix. Dovedale's Stepping Stones appear on a thousand postcards and attract a million visitors, all of whom seem to be queuing to cross the crystal waters of the Dove at the same time. The National Trust does a heroic job to manage this part of its South Peak Estate, but it is still a good idea to keep away from the place on sunny Sundays.

The Dove flows for about 45 miles (72.4km), but only a short section of it is called Dovedale; above the Viator Bridge it becomes Mill Dale, then Wolfscote Dale, then Beresford Dale. But it is to the gorge of Dovedale that the visitors flock, and with good reason, for within the space of 2 or 3 miles (3–5km) of easy riverside walking, on a broad level path, there are superb craggy rocks and pillars (all named) rising out of dense ash woodland, sweeps of open pasture and banks of flowers, dark caves and cascades of spring water. There is no road, and only one main path, following the east (Derbyshire) bank. It is not even necessary to cross the stepping stones upstream from the car park on the Staffordshire side, because there is a footbridge only a few yards away. So visitors can enjoy the best the Peak has to offer in comfort and safety and without doing much damage.

Victorian fashion blighted Dovedale; it was praised by every famous romantic writer from Byron to Tennyson and was soon as popular as Switzerland. Donkey tours and guided expeditions ferried people up the path to view the 'awesome' scenery. Of more enduring merit were the earlier words of Izaak Walton, who loved the Dove and put his head and heart into *The Compleat Angler*. A hotel close to the car park bears his name.

HARTINGTON   Derbyshire Map ref SK1260

Hartington is a tourist honeypot but, like Tissington and Ashford, there is enough in the fabric and culture of the village to cope with popularity and still have a heart. Curiously, its heart is probably the duck pond, or mere, which sits like a round pearl in a circlet of duck-cropped lawn. Close by is Ye Olde Cheeze Shoppe, selling superb local Stiltons. Just a stone's-throw away are tearooms, shops, a pottery and two pubs, old coaching inns from the days when Hartington was a significant market town. One has the unusual name, The Charles Cotton, after the angling resident of Beresford Hall, friend and collaborator of Izaak Walton.

Just out of the village, up a steep side road to the east, is Hartington Hall, built in the 17th century and as sturdy a yeoman's manor as you could wish to see anywhere in the Peak. It was the home of the Bateman family but has been a youth hostel since 1934. Also to the east of the village is a signal box of the Ashbourne–Buxton Railway, which closed in 1967 and is now an information centre on the Tissington Trail, and 3 miles (4.8km) to the north is Pilsbury Castle, now just a mound, probably on the site of an Iron-Age fort.

Hartington occupies a strategic position for walkers and explorers of the less obvious paths and byways. To the east and west lie dry valleys and a lattice of green pastures. To the south is Beresford Dale, the forgotten world of Izaak Walton. It was on the upper reaches of the Dove as it flowed below Beresford Hall that Walton and his friend Charles Cotton perfected their arts and gathered their fishing stories. The fruits of their experience were published in 1653 as *The Compleat Angler*. Cotton was born at Beresford Hall, but spent too much time fishing and writing to earn any money and had to sell the place in 1681. It is now a ruin, though his small 'Fishing Temple' survives on the private west bank, as does the Pike Pool, a quiet shadowy dub on the Dove where a monster pike may yet lurk.

LOCAL CHEESES

The cheese shop at Hartington – Ye Olde Cheeze Shoppe, to use its picturesque title – sells produce from the nearby Hartington Creamery, which was established in the 1870s and began making Stiltons in the 1920s. Specialities include Buxton Blue, White Stilton and Dovedale, a relatively new cheese which is as delicious as any of the more traditional varieties.

Taking a break in the sunshine on the green at Hartington

ILAM PARK

Ilam is the estate village of Ilam Hall, but although it is owned by the National Trust, they lease it to the Youth Hostels Association and it is not open to the public. The lovely parkland which surrounds it is open, though. It was in these grounds that William Congreve wrote his bawdy play *The Old Bachelor* and where Dr Johnson received his inspiration for *Rasselas.* There are delightful walks around the grounds – follow the path in the valley bottom to view the reappearing waters of the Dove and the Manifold.

The distinctive point of Bunster Hill rises above Ilam

ILAM Staffordshire Map ref SK1350

On most maps the River Manifold can be traced in a blue line, flowing south from Wetton to meet the Dove a mile (1.6km) below Ilam. In fact this is not usually what happens, and, like several other celebrated rivers in limestone country, the Manifold is a fugitive and has a secret life, flowing underground unless the water table is high. Below Wetton Mill the river disappears abruptly and takes almost 24 hours to resurface, at the Boil Holes in the grounds of Ilam Hall. This explains why there are no footpaths along what appears on paper to be a pretty section of the lower valley. This does not mean the landscape is not interesting, but there is no clear focal point and the footpaths linking the old halls of Throwley and Castern on the upper slopes of the valley are rarely walked.

Ilam, above the confluence of two famous rivers, has always been an important settlement, but never very large. Originally it belonged to Burton Abbey, but after the Reformation the estate was broken up among three families, the Ports of Ilam Hall, the Meverells of Throwley and the Hurts of Castern. Of these the Meverells no longer exist and Throwley Hall is a ruin; the Ports sold Ilam to Jesse Watts Russell in the early 19th century, and the Hurts still live at secluded Castern.

Alas, Russell swept away most of old Ilam and built a model village, the buildings of which have the look of a Swiss cuckoo clock. Ilam Hall was rebuilt on a grand scale; a quarter of it remains and is used as a youth hostel. Close by is the church, totally rebuilt, but with two fragments from Saxon crosses and a Tudor chapel with a shrine to the local medieval hermit St Bertram.

The Ilam estate passed to the National Trust in 1934 and is a popular destination for day visitors, partly because of its pleasant walks and partly because it is close to Dovedale and has literary associations – with Boswell, Johnson and Izaak Walton.

LONGNOR Staffordshire Map ref SK0864

The fate of little Longnor was sealed by the demise of the turnpikes and the lack of a railway link; its ambition to be a proper market town simply withered. It stands now in the no man's land between the Manifold and the Dove, but at a pivotal point in the National Park, in the very heart of the country. Around it are strip fields dating back to medieval times; less than a mile (1.6km) to the north and east is the Derbyshire border and the start of the limestone country, whilst to the west are the darker hedges and hills of Staffordshire.

The Manifold at Longnor is no more than a babbling brook, but the valley is broad, with meadows and sandstone barns. Yellowhammers and whitethroats sing from the thorn bushes; swallows swoop for insects over the reed-grass. Longnor presides over the long straight road like a drowsy cat over a barn floor. The village is pretty and compact, with a little square and a Victorian market hall. A stone inscription above the entrance carries the tariff of long-forgotten market tolls.

Longnor's market hall is now a crafts centre

A LONG EVENTFUL LIFE
An inscription on a grave in Longnor churchyard:

'In memory of William Billinge, who was born in a Cornfield at Fawfieldhead, in this Parish, in the year 1679. At the age of 23 years he enlisted into His Majesty's Service under Sir George Rooke, and was at the taking of the Fortress of Gibraltar, in 1704. He afterwards served under the Duke of Marlborough at the ever Memorable Battle of Ramilles, on the 23rd of May, 1706, where he was wounded by musket shot in the thigh. He afterwards returned to his native country, and with manly courage defended his Sovereign's rights at the Rebellion in 1715 and 1745. He died within a space of 150 yards of where he was born and was interred here the 30th of January 1791 aged 112 years....'

Footpaths and cycle routes explore the beautiful Manifold Valley

CORAL REEFS OF THE PEAK

The limestone of the Peak District was formed in shallow, tropical seas in Carboniferous times, and because the coral has not dissolved so quickly in rainwater over the last few million years, these reefs now stand as the highest knolls, capping Wetton Hill, Thorpe Cloud and the other white whalebacks of the Dove and Manifold.

MANIFOLD VALLEY Staffordshire Map ref SK1156

The Manifold and the Dove rise within a mile of each other below Axe Edge. As they head southeast together into limestone country, twisting and side-winding like pulled strands of wool, one is transmuted into a Staffordshire valley, the other into a Derbyshire dale. The difference in landscape terms is minimal; they both cut a course through superb scenery, meeting finally at Ilam, yet the Manifold escaped the Victorian hype and still manages to avoid the carnival atmosphere of Dovedale.

Wetton and Warslow villages, on the thousand-foot contour on opposite sides of the valley, are the main access points for the most dramatic section of the Manifold. Neither makes very much concession to tourists, though both have pubs (the Greyhound and the Royal Oak). Warslow has a utilitarian look, as do its iron stocks close to the school. It is an estate village of the Crewe family (of Calke Abbey, south of Derby) and lies at the foot of the gritstone moors, which can be reached by taking the side road to the northwest. Wetton is on the limestone, among dairy farms and barns, but its stout church and many of its cottages look as if they belong among heather.

A steep side road north of Warslow off the B5053 drops down to Ecton, and the most beautiful section of the Manifold begins (see Walk on page 16). It runs south along a narrow strip of level meadow, with steep, flower-studded grassland, almost alpine, on either side. The road, and what is now the Manifold Trail, follows the route of the Leek and Manifold Light Railway, which opened in 1904 but only survived for 30 years; according to expert judgement it opened too late and closed too soon – if its odd Indian-style engines were still running today the line would make a fortune!

Close to Wetton Mill the Manifold usually disappears down swallow-holes, travelling the rest of the way to Ilam underground. Meanwhile, the Manifold's tributary, the Hamps, heads south and the Manifold Trail stays with the old railway line, along the Hamps to Waterhouses.

Out of the depth of the valley, the slopes of the limestone hills are pock-marked with caves. The most famous and dramatic is Thor's Cave but several others such as Ossom's Cave and Elderbush have been explored or excavated and have produced bones and flints from the Stone Age and Bronze Age, when this was good hunting country. All the domed hills (called Lows) are capped by cairns or barrows and it is easy on the dry 'karst' hillsides to imagine yourself in a lost world.

WELL-DRESSING

Well-dressing, the most famous and picturesque of Peak District traditions, probably has its roots in pagan ceremonies to placate water spirits, but the Christian version has its origins at Tissington, where the five wells ran with pure water through the years of the Black Death. The villagers believed they owed their lives to the water, and dressed the wells as a sign of thanksgiving. Well-dressing involves pressing flower petals onto a clay base to create a biblical picture. Many villages dress their wells at different times of the spring or summer.

The river is liable to disappear underground near Wetton Mill, reappearing at Ilam

The pretty estate village of Tissington has given its name to a pathway popular with walkers and cyclists

THE TISSINGTON TRAIL

The famous Tissington Trail runs for 13 miles (20.9km) from Parsley Hey to Ashbourne, along the old railway line which closed in 1963. The trail is particularly suitable for families and cyclists who appreciate a car-free countryside; it is possible to hire bikes at either Parsley Hey or Ashbourne, or bring your own and leave your car behind at the car park, on the site of the old railway station.

TISSINGTON   Derbyshire Map ref SK1752

Tissington is a gem, too beautiful for its own good on summer Sundays but a gift to any photographer. The classic approach is off the A515, through a gateway and over a cattle grid, then along a drive lined with lime trees. The original avenue, of venerable pollards and tall standards, has recently been felled, but there are rows of young trees set further back. Into the village itself, past a walled yew and the first of several wells, sandstone cottages are set behind wide grass verges and shaded by elegant beeches. There is a village green, with the stream running through it, a duck pond complete with ducks, a Norman church and a grand Jacobean Hall. All in all, this is, and has been for centuries, an idyllic, well-managed estate village.

Tissington Hall (not open), low and wide with mullioned windows and tall chimneys, is the home of the Fitzherbert family. Although it is by far the biggest building in the village, it does not impose itself and is set back, behind a low wall and gate of fine wrought ironwork (by Robert Bakewell).

The overwhelming impression of Tissington is of its perfect blend of old stone houses, trees and water. Every wall is draped in flowers and creepers, and everywhere there is the sound of bees. A few decades ago there would have been the sound of steam trains too, but the line closed in 1963 and the grassy trackway is now a famous walk/cycle/horse-riding route, managed by the National Park Authority and known as the Tissington Trail.

A few miles southwest along the Tissington Trail, on the far side of the A515, is the village of Fenny Bentley, an important place to both visitors and residents of Tissington because it has the nearest pub, The Coach and Horses. Fenny Bentley is dominated by a square 15th-century tower, incorporated into the more recent Cherry Orchard Farm. The tower was part of the old Hall, the home of the Beresford family, and in St Edmund's Church is an alabaster tomb to Thomas Beresford and his family. Thomas fought at Agincourt with eight of his sons; these, together with his wife and a further 14 children, are depicted on and around the tomb as bodies tied in shrouds, probably because by the time the tomb was built nobody would have known what they had looked like.

WIRKSWORTH Derbyshire Map ref SK2854

A few years ago Wirksworth was a town of quarry dust and fusty alleys, growing old disgracefully. Now it is one of the most fascinating places to visit in the Peak District, full of history, neat and welcoming. This shows what can happen with a little vision and civic enthusiasm, but there is a suspicion that the hard edges of Wirksworth's past, as a lead-mining and quarrying centre, have been smoothed away rather than dusted off. Of course, lead mining disappeared as an industry many years ago, to be replaced by quarrying, which is still of considerable local importance. A National Stone Centre just out of the town sets the record straight and gives a more rounded picture of this southeast corner of the Peak. Near by is the old quarry of Black Rock, a picnic spot with a 4-mile (6.4-km) forest trail over Cromford Moor and access to the High Peak Trail (the old railway line that transported stone to Cromford Canal).

ANCIENT STONE CARVINGS
St Mary's Church is a treasure-trove of bizarre stone carvings, mostly fragments of Norman masonry in a jigsaw of strange patterns and figures, taken out of context from an older structure and incorporated into the transept walls. But the best carving is on the lid of a Saxon coffin set into the north wall; rows of chunky human figures from a forgotten Byzantine cycle. Enigmatic, unique and usually overlooked.

Displayed in Wirksworth's sturdy Church of St Mary is an unusual carved Anglo-Saxon coffin lid

THE VIRGIN AND THE GYPSY
The little village of Middleton lies on the brow of the hill just north of Wirksworth and there are excellent views across the wooded valley of the Via Gellia. D H Lawrence lived here for a year and featured Middleton (as 'Woodlinkin') in his short novel *The Virgin and the Gypsy*. Near by is Middleton Top, a main access and bike-hire station on the High Peak Trail.

The heart of Wirksworth is the Market Place and car park, from where it is possible to explore the town in several directions. Up Dale End there are wickedly sloping lanes with cobbled gutters, leading past the old smithy, opposite Green Hill, a beautiful 17th-century gabled house built of limestone with sandstone mullioned windows. Further up the hill is Babington House (not open), of similar vintage, set in a pretty garden and with a fine view over the town. It is a more comfortable three-storey residence, with a stone sundial on the gable wall, and its stonework is scrubbed clean and glowing.

South from the Market Place, past the Town Hall, is Coldwell Street with several old inns, including The Red Lion, The Vaults (originally called The Compleat Angler) and The George. Down Chapel Lane is the Moot Hall (not open), the only place in England where lead-miners' Barmote Courts (to settle any lead-mining disputes) are still held (they started here in 1266, though this building only dates back to 1814).

Hidden away from the rest of the town, behind the fronts of tall houses, is St Mary's Church. It sits in its own little world, accessible along Church Street or through the old alley of the lich-gate, of which only the tall stone pillars remain. The grassed churchyard is encircled by iron railings which separate it from a narrow lane called Church Walk and an engaging jumble of back yards and sloping roofs. The church itself seems to have a low centre of gravity, broad and solid and with an eccentrically tiny spire or spike, as if all but the top few feet had fallen through the roof of the tower.

George Eliot set much of her first full-length novel **Adam Bede** *(1859) around Wirksworth*

The Southern Dales

Leisure Information
Places of Interest
Shopping
Sports, Activities
and the Outdoors
Annual Events and Customs

Checklist

Leisure Information

TOURIST INFORMATION CENTRE

Ashbourne
13 The Market Place. Tel: 01335
343666 (Seasonal).

NATIONAL PARK INFORMATION

Peak District National Park Headquarters
Head Office, Aldern House,
Baslow Road, Bakewell.
Tel: 01629 816200.
www.peakdistrict.org.uk

OTHER INFORMATION

Derbyshire Wildlife Trust
Elvaston Castle, Derby.
Tel: 01332 756610.
English Heritage
Canada House, 3 Chepstow
Street, Manchester. Tel: 0161
242 1400.
www. english-heritage.org.uk
English Nature
Manor Barn, Over Haddon,
Bakewell. Tel: 01629 815095.
National Trust
East Midlands Regional Office,
Clumber Park Stableyard,
Worksop, Nottinghamshire.
Tel: 01909 486411.
www.nationaltrust.org.uk

Parking
Visitors' parking tickets are
available to personal callers from
National Park Visitor Centres and
cycle hire centres, or apply In
writing to the Peak District
National Park Head Office at
Bakewell.
Public Transport
The 'Derbyshire Wayfarer' allows
one day's unlimited travel on all
local buses and trains in the
county. Details from Derbyshire
County Council, Public
Transport Dept. Tel: 01629
580000.
Derbyshire Busline Tel: 01298
23098.
GMPTE Tel: 0161 288 7811.
South Yorkshire Travelline
Tel: 01709 515151.
Rail information Tel: 0345
484950.
www.derbysbus.net
Severn Trent Water
2297 Coventry Road,
Birmingham. Tel: 0121
7224968.
Staffordshire Wildlife Trust
Coutts House, Sandon, Stafford.
Tel: 01889 508534.
Weather Call
Tel: 0906 850 0417.
Yorkshire Wildlife Trust
10 Toft Green, York. Tel: 01904
659570.

ORDNANCE SURVEY MAPS

Landranger 1:50,000 Sheets
119, 128.
Outdoor Leisure 1:25,000 Sheet
24.

Places of Interest

There will be an admission
charge at the following places of
interest unless otherwise stated.
Derwent Crystal
Shawcroft, Ashbourne. Tel:
01335 345219. Open all year,
most days. Demonstrations of
glass-blowing Mon–Thu am.
Shop open Mon–Sat all year.
High Peak Junction Workshops
Wirksworth. Tel: 01629 822831.
Original workshops and railway
exhibition and information
centre. Open Easter–Oct, daily;
Nov–Easter, weekends only.
Ilam Park,
4½ miles (7.2km) northwest of
Ashbourne. Woods and parkland
on banks of the River Manifold.
Open all year daily. Free.
Longnor Craft Centre
The Market Hall. Tel: 01298
83587. Open all year daily;
weekends only Jan–Feb.
Middleton Top Engine House
Middleton Top Visitor Centre,

Middleton by Wirksworth.
Tel: 01629 823204. Engine
house with a beam engine to
haul wagons up the Middleton
incline on the Cromford and
High Peak Railway. Open:
Engine house Easter–Oct (engine
in steam on first weekend in the
month); visitor centre weekends
all year, weekdays in summer.

National Stone Centre
Porter Lane, Wirksworth.
Tel: 01629 824833/825403.
Exhibition tells the story of
stone; visitors can try their hand
at gem panning and there are
guided walks. Open all year.

**Steeple Grange Light
Railway**
The Quarry Men's Line,
Middleton by Wirksworth. Tel:
01629 580917. Rides every ten
minutes. Open Easter–Sep Sun
and Bank Hol afternoons only.

Wirksworth Heritage Centre
Crown Yard. Tel: 01629 825225.
Three floors of this former silk
and velvet mill have displays
illustrating the town's past and
present history. Also workshops
showing the skills of
cabinetmakers and a silversmith.
Open: check by phone.

*Wirksworth was formerly a
lead-mining centre*

SPECIAL INTEREST FOR CHILDREN

The following places may be of
interest to visitors with children.
Unless otherwise stated, there
will be an admission charge.

National Stone Centre
Porter Lane, Wirksworth. Tel:
01629 824833/825403.
Exhibition tells the story of
stone; visitors can try their hand
at gem panning and guided
walks are organised. Open all
year.

**Steeple Grange Light
Railway**
The Quarry Men's Line,
Middleton by Wirksworth.
Tel: 01629 55123. Open
Easter–Sep Sun and Bank Hol
afternoons.

Shopping

Ashbourne
Antiques shops in Church Street.
General market Thu; cattle
market on Sat.

Wirksworth
General market Tue.

LOCAL SPECIALITIES

Biscuits
Ashbourne Biscuits. The factory
is not open to the public, but
biscuits can be bought in
Ashbourne.

Cheeses
Local cheeses, including blue
Stilton, from Ye Olde Cheeze
Shoppe, Hartington. Tel: 01298
84935 or the Dove Dairy,
Hartington. Tel: 01298 84496.

Clocks
William Haycock, Clockmaker,
Ashbourne. Tel: 01335 342395.
Established 1826. Workshop
open to public Mon–Fri 9–5.

Crafts
Longnor Craft Centre, The
Market Hall, Longnor.
Tel: 01298 83587.
The work of local craftspeople
and artists are displayed here.
Open all year daily; weekends
only Jan–Feb.

Fresh and Smoked Trout
Mayfield Trout, Manor Farm,
Mayfield. Tel: 01335 342050.
Telephone orders only.

Furniture
Traditional Windsor Armchairs.
Melvyn Tolley, The Old Post
Office, Bradley. Tel: 01335
370112.

Gingerbread
Ashbourne Gingerbread.
Gingerbread can be bought in
Ashbourne.

**Guitars and Hand-crafted
Fretted Instruments**
Noteworthy Musical
Instruments, Main Road,
Hulland Ward. Tel: 01335

370806. Viewing is by appointment only.

Pottery

Rooke's, 1 Mill Lane, Hartington, Tel: 01298 84650.

Sports, Activities and the Outdoors

ANGLING

Fly

Carsington Water, near Ashbourne. Tel: 01629 540478

BOAT HIRE

Carsington Water, near Ashbourne. Tel: 01629 540478.

CYCLING

The High Peak Trail

Starts at Wirksworth and quickly climbs on to high ground where it meets the Tissington Trail at Parsley Hay. For more information contact Derbyshire Countryside Centre. Tel: 01629 823204.

The Manifold Trail

Follows the route of the Leek and Manifold Light Railway, and runs north along the Manifold Valley and river from the A523 near Waterhouses.

The Tissington Trail

Runs for 13½ miles (22km) along part of the old Ashbourne–Buxton railway and the Cromford and High Peak line. The grassy trackway runs alongside Dovedale from Ashbourne, and then climbs to join the High Peak Trail near Parsley Hay for the last mile of the route. Further information from Derbyshire Countryside Centre. Tel: 01629 823204.

CYCLE HIRE

Ashbourne

Ashbourne Cycle Hire Centre, Mapleton Lane. Tel: 01335 343156.

Carsington Water

Tel: 01629 540478.

Middleton Top

Visitor Centre, Middleton by Wirksworth. Tel: 01629 823204.

Parsley Hay

Peak District National Park Centre. Tel: 01298 84493.

Waterhouses

Brown End Farm Cycle Hire.

Tel: 01538 308609.

Peak Cycle Hire, Earls Way, Old Station Car Park. Tel: 01538 308609.

GOLF COURSES

Clifton

Ashbourne Golf Club. Tel: 01335 342078.

GUIDED WALKS

Derbyshire Dales Countryside Service

Planning and Development Services, Town Hall, Matlock. Full guided walks service. Tel: 01629 761100 for details.

National Park Walks with a Ranger

For more details contact the Peak District National Park 24-hour information line Tel: 01629 816327.

Wirksworth

Professional Blue Badge Guides can arrange walks for indiviuals or for parties. Tel: 01629 584284.

HANG-GLIDING

Alston Field

Adrenaline High Adventure Sports, the Old Vicarage, Wetton, near Ashbourne. Tel: 01335 310296.

Ashbourne

The Peak School of Hang Gliding, The Elms, Wetton. Tel: 01335 310257.

LONG-DISTANCE FOOTPATHS AND TRAILS

The High Peak Trail

Starts at Wirksworth and meets the Tissington Trail at Parsley Hay. For information contact Derbyshire Countryside Centre. Tel: 01629 823204.

Manifold Valley Visitor Centre

Hulme End. Housed in a former ticket office of Leek and Manifold Light Railway. Direct access to the Manifold Track which offers 8¼ miles (13km) of walking or cycling from Hulme End to Waterhouses. Tel: 01298 84679.

The Tissington Trail

Part of old Ashbourne–Buxton railway and Cromford and High Peak line. Runs alongside

Dovedale from Ashbourne, and joins the High Peak Trail near Parsley Hay. For information contact Derbyshire Countryside Centre. Tel: 01629 823204.

SAILING

Carsington Water, near Ashbourne. Tel: 01629 540478.

WATERSPORTS

Carsington Water, near Ashbourne. Tel: 01629 540478.

Annual Events and Customs

Ashbourne

Shrovetide Football (Shrove Tuesday–Ash Wednesday). Wynaston Show and Gymkhana, early June.

Official World Toe Wrestling Championships, Wetton, early June.

Highland Gathering, with parade of pipe bands, mid-July. Ashbourne Show, late August.

Dovedale

The Dovedale Dash, a 4¼-mile (6.8km) cross-country run which starts on Thorpe Pastures.

Hartington

Derbyshire Steam Fair, Hartington Moor showground, late May.

Derbyshire Country Show, Hartington Moor showground, late August.

Ilam

Manifold Valley Agricultural Show, The Arbour, Castern Hall Farm, early August. Dovedale Sheepdog Trials, mid-August.

Longnor

Well-dressing and Wakes, early September.

Longnor Races, early September.

Tissington

Well-dressing, Ascension Day.

Wirksworth

Well-dressing, late May. Clypping of the Church service, early September. Festival of Music and Arts, early/late September.

Further information can be obtained from Tourist Information Centres.

Buxton and the Western Moors

The silk towns of Macclesfield and Leek mark the western and southern edges of the Peak uplands: to the north are Whaley Bridge and Chapel-en-le-Frith. In-between is the least explored section of the Peak District, yet one of the most fascinating. Dramatic gritstone outcrops and windswept heather moors stretch as far as the eye can see to the east. From the elegant hilltops of Shining Tor and Shutlingsloe, from old pastureland of Wincle Minn and the ancient forest chapel of St Stephens. Two rivers drain the watershed: to the north the Goyt, rising on the peaty slopes of the Cat and Fiddle Moor; to the south the pretty River Dane. To the east of all this is the grand spa town of Buxton.

THE BEST BREW

Local people still queue up at St Ann's Well to fill plastic containers with the tepid water, claiming it makes the best tea in Britain. Try it straight from the well. It was good enough for Mary, Queen of Scots, and it was what brought the Romans here in the first place.

Taking the waters at St Ann's Well

BUXTON Derbyshire Map ref SK0572

Dropping down from the high moors into the spa town of Buxton is enough to make anyone blink in disbelief as they find themselves emerging out of the bleak wilderness into a bower of parks and gardens and grand Palladian-style buildings.

Through the centuries health resorts have sprung up in all sorts of unlikely places, and none more so than Buxton. The Romans, who had a passion for bathing, established a rest or leisure facility here in the days of Agricola, when the frontier fighting had shifted north to Caledonia and this was a safe haven with natural warm springs. After the Romans came the Christians, who took the 'cripple's cure' at St Ann's Well and prayed for miracles.

By the 18th century Buxton, in common with other spa towns, was on the fashion trail. The 5th Duke of Devonshire was responsible for the main wave of building innovation at Buxton. He had been impressed in the 1770s by the Royal Crescent at Bath and was awash with money from his Manifold copper mines. First he had the elegant semi-circular Crescent built, complete with 42 pilasters and 378 windows, then the Great Stable with a central court and Tuscan columns, then Hall Bank and The Square, all of a grand and imposing style.

In the 19th century the 6th and 7th Dukes carried on

the work, so that by late Victorian times the spa in the valley had completely eclipsed the old market town on the upper slope. The Great Stable became the Devonshire Hospital, 'for the use of the sick poor', and was given a massive domed roof 156 feet (47.4m) across; terraces of hotels and guesthouses sprang up to cater for the influx of affluent visitors to the Thermal and Natural Baths; the railways arrived, the beautiful Pavilion Gardens were laid out on the banks of the Wye, and in 1905 the Opera House was opened.

Surprisingly, the majority of Buxton's fine buildings are still functioning and thriving. The Edwardian Opera House has a full programme, taking advantage of the current interest in opera. Outside is an immaculate square, complete with an ornate Victorian postbox, and behind it run the Pavilion Gardens, complete with a Serpentine Walk.

Perhaps the best way to absorb Buxton's authentic atmosphere is to park at the market place in the old town (which still claims to be the highest market town in England) and walk past the town hall, down a path across the grassy dome called The Slopes towards the Crescent. Few places in England evoke such a comfortable, Victorian Pre-Raphaelite sense of town and country. Shopping arcades keep the streets lively and there is an Information Centre on the site of the original mineral baths. Opposite The Crescent is the old Pump Room, where visitors once took their prescribed mineral waters. Near by stands a modest fountain, the source of the famous waters and of Buxton's continued prosperity.

HEATHER ON THE MOORS
Common heather, or ling, turns the moors purple in August, but there are two other kinds of heather on the hills around Buxton – cross-leaved heath on wet or boggy ground and bell-heather on dry rocky slopes. Both these plants have bigger flowers than common heather, but don't attract so many bees. Heather honey is a local speciality, wonderful on new bread.

The grand Opera House becomes a focus of attention during Buxton's popular summer music festival

The well-weathered town stocks still stand in the square at Chapel-en-le-Frith

BRUTAL TIMES

One morbid episode in Chapel's history casts a long shadow. In the Civil War, following the Battle of Ribbleton Moor in 1648, 1,500 Scottish soldiers were imprisoned in the church for 16 days. The conditions must have been appalling. By the time they were let out, to start a forced march north, 44 men were dead. They were buried in the churchyard, a testament to brutal times.

CHAPEL-EN-LE-FRITH Derbyshire Map ref SK0580

A pretty name does not always describe a pretty place. The frith, or forest, never really existed except to formalise a vast Norman hunting preserve; most of the Derbyshire countryside was open ground rather than woodland.

The most obvious feature of Chapel today is its dowdy main road, sweeping south into a hollow and on towards Buxton. A bypass now carries A6 traffic around to the east, but it will take some years for this part of Chapel to brighten up. However, turning off the main road at the white-painted Kings Arms at the top of the town, brings you directly to the market place and a delightful change of character. Cobbled paths and a medieval cross and stocks stand at the heart of the little square, overlooked by a café called The Stocks. Except on market day (Thursday) this is a quiet and out of the way place, perfect for a cup of tea and a wander. Close by is the Roebuck Inn, and a little way along the street, opposite the church, is what was once the Bulls Head Inn, of which only the head, a fine life-size shorthorn bull's head, still survives.

St Thomas à Becket Church stands on a grassy knoll overlooking a new housing estate. The original chapel in the forest was built here around 1225, but was replaced in the early 14th century by a more sturdy structure. Most of what is visible today is from the refurbishment of 1733, but there are hints of antiquity all around; the shaft of a Saxon cross, a weathered sundial, and a view across what must have been glorious hunting country.

THE GOYT VALLEY Cheshire Map ref SK0075

The River Goyt meets the Mersey at Stockport and never gets the chance to grow into anything fierce. Its few miles of splendour lie in its upper reaches, bounded by high winding roads on the Derbyshire–Cheshire border. Considering the closeness of industrial towns, this empty rolling land is a real delight; the moorland is among the finest in the Peak District, and in late summer the purple of the heather can be breathtaking.

The Goyt flows from south to north; it rises on the slopes of Cat and Fiddle Moor, a wild and windswept place with a reputation for the worst of weather. The moor is named after the Cat and Fiddle Inn, one of the highest and loneliest pubs in England. Like other high-altitude hostelries, such as The Snake or Tan Hill, it was built in the turnpike era at the start of the 19th century and is still a welcome sight for traffic on the sinuous A537. There are no other houses for miles around, but some visitor facilities are available at Derbyshire Bridge, which is the usual starting point for people exploring the valley.

Years ago the Goyt was as near a natural upland valley as is possible in England, but the original scatter of ancient oaks has now been augmented or replaced by conifer plantations and the river and meadows have been flooded to create Fernilee and Errwood Reservoirs (see Walk on page 36). The combination of lake and forest, cobalt and viridian beneath the magenta of heather moorland, rising to the highest point in Cheshire at Shining Tor, 1,834 feet (559m), makes the Goyt a colourful and classy place; parking and picnic sites around the reservoir shores and the walks through the woodland draw so many visitors that there is a one-way system up the narrow road to Derbyshire Bridge.

GOYT MOSS

Below Cat and Fiddle Moor is Goyt Moss, a colourful carpet of cotton grass and asphodel belying a treacherous surface of wet peat. In late April and May golden plovers and curlews add their voices to those of pipits and larks; this is also the breeding ground of the twite, a small finch, darker than a linnet and with a pink rump.

The moorland around Goyt's Moss and Cat and Fiddle Moor is some of the wildest in England

A Buxton Figure of Eight

An attraction in its own right, Buxton lies at the heart of outstanding countryside, and high roads with magnificent views radiate from it. This tour makes the most of the town's situation with a figure-of-eight route, out on the shoulder of the Goyt, back via Chapel-en-le-Frith and Dove Holes, then out again on the dramatic Axe Edge road and down towards Leek, before returning through quiet rolling farmland.

ROUTE DIRECTIONS

See Key to Car Tours on page 120.

Start in Buxton, in front of the Devonshire Royal Hospital. Follow the A5004 to the left, sweeping uphill for a mile (1.6km) through woodland and then over moorland. After another half mile (0.8km) a cairn on the right marks the National Park boundary.

Continue for 2½ miles (4km) along the shoulder of the valley to the Upper Hall lay-by (wonderful views). Drive on for another 2 miles (3.2km), through Fernilee, to the outskirts of Whaley Bridge, where you turn right along the B5470, signed Chapel-en-le-Frith. Go over the bridge and on for another 3 miles (4.8km) through Tunstead

Milton to enter Chapel-en-le-Frith. (Turn off at the Kings Arms, on the left, if you want to explore the town.)

Drive along the B5470 through Chapel-en-le-Frith for another mile (1.6km), past the Packhorse on the left, then turn left following the sign for the A6 and Buxton. Turn right to join the A6, along a wooded valley for 2 miles (3.2km) to Dove Holes. This workaday quarry village hides the site of a prehistoric henge. Continue on the A6 for 3 miles (4.8km) to Fairfield, a pretty village on the outskirts of Buxton. The road descends into the middle of Buxton; at the bottom, follow the signs for the A53 to Leek, via four roundabouts but well signed, with the dome of the Devonshire Hospital soon visible ahead.

Back at the hospital, begin

The spa at Buxton, England's highest town, was first exploited by the Romans

the second loop of the tour by following the A53 'signed' Leek, passing the Pavilion Gardens on the left. Continue uphill out of town for 2 miles (3.2km), through traffic lights and out on to open hilltops – the start of Axe Edge. The Dove and Manifold rise here.

The road gradually descends past a side road to the village of Flash and out of Derbyshire into Staffordshire, then on for about 3 miles (4.8km) to **Ramshaw Rocks** on the right. These include a rock which looks like a face.

Continue on the A53 for another 1½ miles (2.4km), down to Upper Hulme and Blackshaw Moor and off the high moorland. In 2 miles (3.2km) pass the Moss Rose Inn, then in less than half a mile (0.8km) turn left on to Springfield Road, signed 'Ashbourne'. Shortly reach a junction with the A52 (A523); turn right to visit Leek or left to continue the tour, on the A52 (A523) signed 'Ashbourne' and 'Derby'.

Head uphill through rolling pastureland for 2½ miles (4km) and pass a turn to the RSPB Nature Reserve of **Coombes Valley**, then on for 1½ miles (2.4km) to Bottom House crossroads and the Green Man Inn. Turn left along the B5053 signed 'Longnor' and continue for 1½ miles (2.4km) through Onecote. After 2½ miles (4km) the road twists down to cross the pretty Warslow Brook, a tributary of the Manifold, then rises for a mile (1.6km) to the village of Warslow.

Continue along the B5053 for 4 miles (6.4km), crossing the River Manifold to climb sharply into Longnor, a compact and attractive village amidst farming country. Bear left, up out of the village, then on for a mile (1.6km) to cross the River Dove at Glutton

Bridge, back into Derbyshire. The landscape changes quite abruptly as the road follows a limestone gorge (Glutton Dale) for half a mile (0.8km) up to a crossroads (Dalehead to the left, Earl Sterndale to the right). Go straight on, as the road curves to the left

beneath a steep bank and rises for 1½ miles (2.4km) past the working quarries at Hind Low to a T-junction at Brierlow Bar. Turn left on to the A515 and drive for 3 miles (4.8km) to return to Buxton town centre and the start point of the drive.

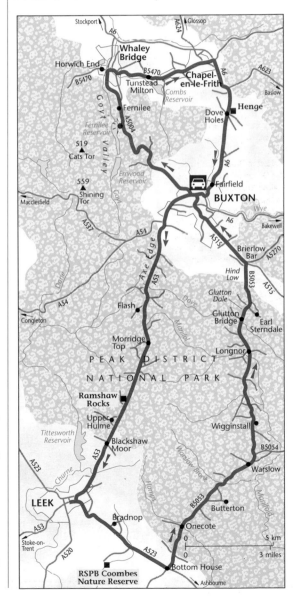

Goyt Valley and Shining Tor

This walk begins at the small southern reservoir, Errwood, and climbs through attractive woodland to the spectacular gritstone ridge to Shining Tor, then descends along Goyt's Clough at the head of the valley.

Time: about 4 hours. Distance: 7 miles (11.3km).
Location: 3 miles (4.8km) northwest of Buxton.
Start: From Buxton on the A5004, then left down the side road (signed Goyt) and between the reservoirs, then turn left to the car park at the southern end of Errwood Reservoir.
(OS Grid ref: SK012748.)
OS Map: Outdoor Leisure 24
(The Peak District – White Peak area) 1:25,000.
See Key to Walks on page 121.

ROUTE DIRECTIONS

Start along a woodland walk from the rear of the car park – away from **Errwood Reservoir**. Take the right fork of two grassy paths to a gap through a wall, then turn right down a wooded track. At another 'Woodland Walk' sign turn sharp right and curve left past the ruins of **Errwood Hall**. Go on alongside a stream on the right, cross it and another path at right angles, and climb gradually ahead on a concessionary path leaving the stream below on the left. Ignore a path turning right into a wood. The '**Spanish**

Looking to the northwest from Pym Chair

Shrine' is passed near the head of the valley. Soon after, keep left at another path junction and join a road. Follow the footpath on the right of the road to the crest at **Pym Chair**. There are excellent views, north and east into the High Peak and west over the Cheshire Plain. Turn left, cross a stile and follow the ridge alongside a wall on the right. Keep along the ridge for about 2 miles (3.2km), ignoring a path to the right near to the summit.

From the summit of Shining Tor turn left, still keeping the wall on the right. Descend into a shallow valley then up to the next ridge. Cross a stile, turn right along the ridge and cross a stile. In 50 yards (46m) when three paths diverge, turn sharp left, signed 'Goyts Clough'. Keeping a wall on the left, walk downhill skirting the edge of the conifer plantation, then enter it at a stile. Go down through the trees to a little valley. Cross the stream and angle up left, taking the right fork to an old

gatepost and along a broad path curving right through conifers. A stile leads out of the forest. Turn sharp left. Foxlow Edge is in view ahead – the outward route runs just below it.

Walk down to a road which runs by **Goyt's Moss** and up the little valley called **Goyt's Clough** and turn left along it. Just after a parking area turn right opposite a gate, descend steeply to the River Goyt and follow it downstream.

The path rises to meet the road again. Go straight across to a gate and follow a track, signposted 'Errwood Hall', above the road. Continue along the track when a path turns right, go through large gateposts into a conifer plantation and turn right through the next gateway to the car park at the start of the walk.

POINTS OF INTEREST

Errwood Reservoir
The Goyt Reservoirs look as if they have always been here, but they are a recent addition to the landscape, constructed by Stockport Corporation. Fernilee, to the north, was flooded in 1938 and the Errwood scheme followed in 1967. Woodland plantations were added by the Forestry Commission in the 1960s.

Errwood Hall
Errwood Hall was built by the Grimshawe family in 1830 to an Italian design and the grounds were planted with azaleas and rhododendrons. The building was demolished prior to the flooding of Fernilee but the now neglected rhododendrons remain.

The Spanish Shrine
This little stone building,

with a beehive roof is kept in good condition. It was built by the Grimshawes as a memorial to their Spanish governess and companion, Miss Dolores.

Pym Chair and the Ridge

The west–east path, called The Street, which crosses the gritstone ridge at Pym Chair, is an old salters' road, used by packhorse trains loaded with salt from the Cheshire Plain. Cats Tor gets its name from the wild cats which once lived here. Shining Tor is the highest point of the ridge at 1,834 feet (559m), with fine views south, dominated by the cone of Shutlingsloe, 1,670 feet (509m).

Goyt's Clough and Moss

The mixed woodland along the tumbling River Goyt is a habitat for several scarce species of songbirds, most notably the redstart and the wood warbler. The rocky outcrops are the home of the ring ouzel, and the beautiful heather-covered moors echo to the mournful calls of golden plovers and curlews. These birds are all summer visitors to the Goyt; in winter there are only the crows and a few grouse.

A venerable butter cross stands at the heart of Leek

'SCHEMER' BRINDLEY

James Brindley, Leek's most famous son, was actually born at Wormhill, near Tideswell, but his family moved to Leek in 1726 when he was ten. He was apprenticed to a millwright at Sutton, near Macclesfield, when he was 17 and was soon solving all sorts of engineering problems. Most of his ideas worked, and he was nicknamed 'Schemer'. Wealth and notoriety followed, but in his later years he became famous for his canal designs, particularly the Trent and Mersey and its Harecastle Tunnel. Brindley died from pneumonia in 1772.

LEEK Staffordshire Map ref SJ9856

The little Staffordshire mill town of Leek sits comfortably on a broad low hill in a curve of the River Churnet. Unlike most of the other towns circling the Peak District, Leek is not overshadowed by the hills and makes no great claims to be an adventure centre. All around are green valleys and rolling pastures, full of dairy cattle and longwool sheep. To the south lies the Churnet, with a host of visitor attractions such as the Cheddleton Railway Centre, the old Cheddleton Flint Mill and the Caldon Canal. To the southwest, out of sight and out of mind, is Stoke-on-Trent. But to the north and east the foothills rise inexorably to heather moorland and limestone plateaux; like Macclesfield and Glossop there is a sense of a settlement butting as closely to the hills as it dared, exploiting the power of the elements.

Textiles transformed Leek from a medieval market town to an industrial sprawl, but silk was the speciality, which meant that many of the early mills were small and clean, with better working conditions than those endured in the cotton mills of the Peak valleys. Most of the mill buildings are now put to other uses, and the red-brick and half-timbered houses of the town might belong anywhere.

The heart of old Leek, easily missed on a fleeting visit, is the cobbled Market Place. At one end of it stands the 17th-century Butter Cross, a link with the town's dairying tradition. The cross was removed from its original location, at the lower side of the square towards Sheep Market, nearly two centuries ago and has been restored. A pretty watermill stands at the edge of Leek as a monument to the persistence of James Brindley, the 18th-century canal engineer. Further upstream, a tributary of the Churnet was dammed to create Rudyard Lake, to supply water for his Trent and Mersey Canal. A few miles to the east, the Churnet itself has been dammed to form Tittesworth Reservoir, with typical water authority facilities, including a visitor centre, woodland walks, car parks, angling and a bird hide overlooking the shallow northern corner.

LYME PARK   Cheshire Map ref SJ9784

Lyme Park (National Trust) on the western edge of the Peak National Park is a modest mirror-image of Chatsworth. The exterior, made grimy by the smoky air of Manchester, is Palladian in style, the work of the Italian architect Giacomo Leoni. The interior, housing family portraits and a collection of clocks, is essentially Elizabethan but with many additions and alterations.

Lyme was the home of the Legh family for 600 years and has sufficient style to make it one of the top visitor attractions in the area, set in a rural idyll of gardens, parkland and moorland, yet only a stone's throw from Stockport. Those who prefer outdoor attractions to the splendours of the stately home will enjoy the wildfowl on the lake and herds of red and fallow deer among the trees. The 1,300-acre park also has excellent short walks and viewpoints: a modest alternative to the high hills if the weather is closing in.

SILKEN THREADS
With Leek's textile industry specialising in silk, it was an appropriate place for the setting up of a School of Needlework, founded by Elizabeth Wardle, later Lady Wardle, in 1870. The Victorian craftswomen of the Leek Embroidery Society produced a full-size replica of the Bayeux Tapestry, but if you want to see it, you will have to go all the way to Reading in Berkshire, where it is a prized possession of the Reading Museum.

The regular features of Lyme Park's south front are perfectly reflected in the lake

THE COUNTRY ARTIST

Charles Tunnicliffe, one of the best-known country artists of the 20th century, was born and raised on a farm at Sutton Lane Ends, a few miles southeast of Macclesfield. The farm was within sketching distance of dramatic Peak District scenery, but most of Tunnicliffe's paintings at that time were of cattle and horses and the patchwork of family farms on the shoulder of the hills. His distant views were to the west, over the Cheshire Plain. Anyone visiting this area for the first time may feel they are already familiar with the landscape, having seen it in the background of Ladybird books, tea cards or RSPB prints.

A memorial to its founder, John Whitaker, in front of Macclesfield's splendid former Sunday School

MACCLESFIELD   Cheshire Map ref SJ9173

The town of Macclesfield sits firmly at the foot of the hills, close enough to suffer draughts of frost-laden air and share any low cloud. Specialising in silk was its salvation and its downfall. From a market town, Macclesfield first became known for buttons, then for all kinds of silken products. By the mid-19th century the town was bursting at the seams, with 56 silk 'throwsters' (producing the thread or thrown silk) and 86 businesses creating silk fabric or finished goods. Despite this success, or perhaps because of it, the workforce lived in wretched conditions, with an appalling level of infant mortality, and with nowhere to go when the industry hit one of its frequent declines.

Silk mills, chapels and banks, solid square buildings of blackened stone, are scattered through the town today. Among them is the huge Sunday School on Roe Street which is now a heritage centre with a silk museum and shop. Near the old market cross, behind St Michael's Church and its beautiful soot-covered chapel of 1501, lies a narrow garden terrace known as Sparrow Park (officially, the Broadhurst Memorial Gardens). This is a pivot of the old town, a place to stop and ponder its chequered history. Below the gardens there is a steep bank, down which run the picturesque 108 Steps. There is a view through the shrubs of the railway station and over the anonymous hinterland of the town, to green remembered foothills at the western face of the Peak.

On the rising farmland of the foothills, above Sutton Lane Ends and a growing patchwork of housing estates, lie the two Langley Reservoirs. They were built in the mid-19th century to provide clean water for Macclesfield, as a response to infant mortality and disease among the mill workers. But young Charles Tunnicliffe, the famous country artist, knew them in more peaceful times as a haunt of herons and moorhens. Further into the hills are Ridgegate and Trentabank reservoirs, the winter resort of pochard and goldeneye. Then comes the conifer blanket of Macclesfield Forest, once part of a vast royal hunting forest.

Close to Trentabank is a Forest Visitor Centre, from where there are walks and drives. At the northern edge of the forest lies the tiny Chapel of St Stephen, where a rush-bearing ceremony takes place each August. And at the highest southern access point there is a path which leads out on to open moorland, up to Shutlingsloe, one of the most distinctive and shapely of Peak summits.

About 3 miles (4.8km) south of Macclesfield is Gawsworth Hall, a fine Tudor black-and-white manor house which was the birthplace of Mary Fitton. This renowned lady is thought by some to be the 'Dark Lady' of Shakespeare's sonnets, who aroused such emotional turmoil in the poet. We shall probably never know, but the house is worth a visit anyway, for its wonderful old timberwork, its paintings and suits of armour. The grounds, thought to be a rare example of an Elizabethan pleasure garden, include a tilting ground and are the venue for open-air theatre and craft fairs during the summer months.

Trentabank Reservoir nestles in the hills east of Macclesfield

TEGG'S NOSE AND THE GRITSTONE TRAIL

The best introduction to the Cheshire slice of the Peak landscape is from Tegg's Nose Country Park, along Buxton Old Road to the east of Macclesfield. There are superb views from the Windy Way car park and walks along a network of tracks and pathways, by the old quarry or down through woodland to the reservoirs above Langley. It is possible at this point to join the Gritstone Trail, a long-distance footpath running from Lyme Park to Rushton Spencer.

BEYOND THE LAW

Below Cut-thorn Hill lies Three Shires Head, where a packhorse bridge stands at the cusp between Derbyshire, Cheshire and Staffordshire. Years ago, this was where illegal prize fights took place because local police forces had no authority to pursue suspects beyond their own county boundary. For the same reason, Flash became the capital of coin counterfeiting, and the word Flash ('Flash Harry', 'flash money' etc) entered the language to denote a fake.

THE ROACHES Staffordshire

There are few real peaks in the Peak District (the name is derived from the Old English *peac*, meaning a hill of any sort), but the most elegant and craggy-topped are those of the far west: Hen Cloud, Ramshaw Rocks and The Roaches. They are gritstone outcrops, similar to those making up the Dark Peak and the Eastern Moors, but on this side they were more heavily contorted or squashed together, leading to a landscape of misfit valleys, steep slopes and rock faces rather than plateau moorland.

Ramshaw Rocks are probably the best-known outlier of the Roaches, simply because they tower above the roadside on the A53 north of Leek and display a feature like a face, complete with an eye that winks at you as you drive north. The A53 and the quiet winding roads to the west of Axe Edge always seem to lead to interesting places, forgotten or undiscovered.

Axe Edge itself is too high to be anything but wild. One notable village tucked away just off the main road is Flash, which proclaims itself the highest village in England at 1,518 feet (462.7m). The River Dane rises near by, jinking a course between hills and ridges and flowing southwest to Gradbach (see Walk on page 44) and Danebridge: this is delightful countryside full of trees and meadows, old barns and cowslip banks.

The Roaches ridge lies a few miles to the southwest of Flash and runs northwest/southeast, its main rock-climbing exposures facing the setting sun. A footpath follows the crest of the ridge, linking with Back Forest and creating a 4-mile (6.4-km) ridge walk with superb views. Heather clothes the upper hills, bracken and woodland the slopes. The area has become famous as the home of a colony of red-necked wallabies, a Tasmanian oddity which arrived at Roaches Hall via Whipsnade in the 1930s and escaped to form a feral population.

The magnificent tilted ridge of The Roaches, with Hen Cloud beyond

WHALEY BRIDGE   Derbyshire Map ref SK0180

This little town (or large village) grew up with dust on its face and Goyt water in its veins. Coal and textiles provided the only gainful work, and both have now gone. These days there is hardly a whisper of past industry and employment is more varied. Visitors call in on their way to the Goyt Valley or the Peak Forest Canal.

Just out of Whaley Bridge, above Bing Wood (a 'bing' is a slag heap) is the curious scooped-out ridge called Roosdyche. It was once described as a Roman racecourse, on purely visual evidence – nobody could explain who or what else could have created such a flat-bottomed valley. The answer, of course, was ice.

South of the town is Toddbrook Reservoir, built to feed the Peak Forest Canal, and Taxal, a tiny village clustered around its church. Inside St James's are memorials to the Jodrell family, and a monument to Michael Heathcote, 'Gentleman of the Pantry and Yeoman of the Mouth to His Late Majesty King George the Second'. Heathcote lived to be 75, so presumably nobody tried to poison the king in his time as official food-taster.

WILDBOARCLOUGH   Cheshire Map ref SJ9868

Only a few outbuildings remain of the three mills that once made the valley of Clough Brook a significant annexe to the Macclesfield silk industry. James Brindley made his reputation here at the turn of the 19th century, and in their heyday the mills found work for 600 people.

Along the valley today most traces of industry are camouflaged green. There are shrub-covered foundations, grassy trackways and mossy walls. The stream boasts pretty waterfalls and deep pools and is the territory of dippers and grey wagtails. The impression is of a rural backwater, at the foot of Shutlingsloe, the 'Cheshire Matterhorn'.

WILD COUNTRY

It is difficult to imagine this sweep of country as a dangerous wilderness, but names on the map like Wolf End and Wildboarclough hint at the reputation it once enjoyed. Whether the last English boar was really killed here is open to question. These days you are more likely to see a wallaby than a wolf.

Longboats on the Peak Forest Canal at Whaley Bridge offer a leisurely way to view the countryside

Back Forest and Lud's Church

This corner of the Peak District was part of the
Macclesfield Forest, and the gritstone ridge of Back
Forest bears a canopy of bracken and heather rather
than trees. The views from the ridge crest are
outstanding, and the path winds along the valley of
the River Dane and through the wooded lower slopes.
Halfway down the hill lies Lud's Church, a chasm in the
gritstone with mists of an Arthurian
legend heavy in the air.

Time: about 3 hours. Distance: 5 miles (8km).
Location: 8 miles (12.9km) southwest of Buxton.
Start: From Buxton take the A54, turn left in 7 miles (11.2km)
along a side road at the Rose and Crown inn and park at the
Peak National Park car park near Gradbach Mill.
(OS Grid ref: SJ998662.)
OS Map: Outdoor Leisure 24
(The Peak District – White Peak area) 1:25,000.
See Key to Walks on page 121.

ROUTE DIRECTIONS

Turn right out of the car park
and walk along the road to
Gradbach Mill, now a youth
hostel. Near the front entrance
of the hostel bear left and
climb the path to a stile. Go
through this and walk along
the edge of a field to another
stile. Turn left after this, along
a lane, following the River
Dane downstream. When the
lane bears left go through a
stile on the right and cross a
footbridge. Turn left along
Black Brook, ignoring a
junction, after which the path
climbs up through a wood
above the Brook. The gradient
steepens near the edge of the
conifers. Continue ahead,
signed 'Roach End', going
down into a dip then climbing
up on to open moorland,
approaching a wall and
following this to the top.
At the crest of the ridge,

turn right over a stile then
turn right to cross another
stile by a gate. With splendid
views on all sides, walk on
along the ridge beside a wall
on the left. Keep on the ridge
when the wall and another
path veer left downhill.

Go straight ahead at a path
crossroads, still keeping along
the ridge, with a wall now on
the right for a while. After the
last rock outcrop at the end of
the ridge, with views of
Wincle Minn and the **River
Dane** to the west, descend to
another path junction. Turn
right and continue to descend
beside a wall, keeping straight
ahead when the wall turns
left. At a large rock outcrop
take the right fork and explore
the deep narrow gorge
known as **Lud's Church**.
Retrace your steps to the big
rock and continue downhill
through the woods until the

confluence of the two streams
comes into view. Turn down
to the footbridge and follow
the outward route back to the
youth hostel and the car park.

POINTS OF INTEREST

Gradbach Mill
The original Gradbach silk
mill burned down in 1785;
it was rebuilt as a flax mill,
then as a sawmill, and is
now a youth hostel. The
giant waterwheel is long
gone, as are the cottages
that housed the workforce.
The ponds were used to
gather iron-stained
floodwater from the River
Dane. The water was then
left to evaporate, leaving
bright orange ochre which
was sent to Manchester. Raw
ochre was also used in sheep
dips to colour the fleeces
before market.
   Along the lane close to the
mill is a fine gritstone horse
trough, fed by a spring and
with seats at either end.
Workhorses may have used
the trough, but it is unlikely
that ploughboys were
allowed to sit idly by.

The Roaches
A dramatic millstone grit
outcrop, famous for rock-
climbing and for its feral
population of wallabies.

**Wincle Minn and the
River Dane**
From the Wincle Minn
viewpoint you are looking
west over the River Dane as
it gathers itself for a wander
over the Cheshire Plain.
Danebridge lies on this side
of the river, and Wincle,
with its pretty scatter of
farms and cottages, lies on
the other. The ridge a mile
beyond Wincle, above the
tributary stream of the Shell
Brook, is known either as
Wincle Minn or Bosley
Minn, depending on

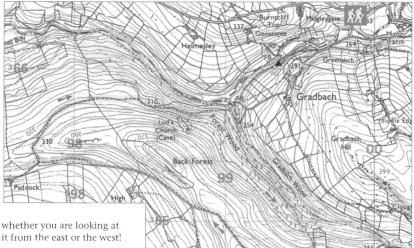

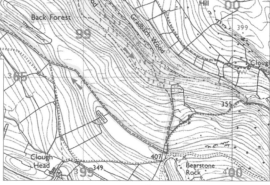

whether you are looking at it from the east or the west!

Lud's Church

This extraordinary natural chasm has a dubious reputation. In the 14th century it was the meeting place of an heretical cult of dissenters called the Lollards. More romantically,

Looking over to Gradbach from Burntcliffe

or fancifully, it was the place where Gawain fought the Green Knight in the medieval epic tale. Not

surprisingly, Victorian travellers found it an awful place and were thoroughly frightened.

Buxton and The Western Moors

Leisure Information

Places of Interest

Shopping

The Performing Arts

Checklist Sports, Activities and
the Outdoors

Annual Events and Customs

Leisure Information

TOURIST INFORMATION CENTRES

Buxton
The Crescent. Tel: 01298 25106.
Leek
Market Place. Tel: 01538
483741.
Macclesfield
Council Offices, Town Hall.
Tel: 01625 504114.

NATIONAL PARK INFORMATION

Peak District National Park Headquarters
Head Office, Aldern House,
Baslow Road, Bakewell.
Tel: 01629 816200.
www.peakdistrict.org.uk

OTHER INFORMATION

Cheshire Wildlife Trust
Grebe House, Reaseheath,
Nantwich, Cheshire. Tel: 01270
610180.
Derbyshire Wildlife Trust
Elvaston Castle, Derby.
Tel: 01332 756610.
English Heritage
Canada House, 3 Chepstow
Street, Manchester. Tel: 0161
242 1400.
www. english-heritage.org.uk
English Nature
Manor Barn, Over Haddon,

Bakewell. Tel: 01629 815095.
National Trust
East Midlands Regional Office,
Clumber Park Stableyard,
Worksop, Nottinghamshire.
Tel: 01909 486411.
Lyme Park, Disley, Cheshire.
Tel: 01663 762023.
www.nationaltrust.org.uk
North West Water
Dawson House, Great Sankey,
Warrington, Cheshire.
Tel: 01925 234000.
Public Transport
The 'Derbyshire Wayfarer' allows
one day's unlimited travel on all
local buses and trains in the
county. Details from Derbyshire
County Council, Public
Transport Dept. Tel: 01629
580000.
Derbyshire Busline Tel: 01298
23098.
GMPTE Tel: 0161 288 7811.
South Yorkshire Travelline Tel:
01709 515151.
Rail information Tel: 0345
484950.
www.derbysbus.net
Severn Trent Water
2297 Coventry Road,
Birmingham,
West Midlands.
Tel: 0121 722 4768.
Staffordshire Wildlife Trust
Coutts House, Sandon, Stafford.
Tel: 01889 508534.

Weather Call
Tel: 0906 850 0417.

ORDNANCE SURVEY MAPS

Landranger 1:50,000 Sheets
118, 119.
Outdoor Leisure 1:25,000
Sheets 1, 24.

Places of Interest

There will be an admission
charge at the following places
of interest unless otherwise
stated.
Brindley Mill
Mill Street, Leek. Tel: 01538
483741. Open Easter–Sep
weekends and Bank Hol Mon;
Jul and Aug limited opening.
Buxton Museum and Art Gallery
Peak Buildings, Terrace Road.
Tel: 01298 24658. Archaeology,
geology, etc. Open all year,
most days.
Cheddleton Flint Mill
Beside Caldon Canal, Leek
Road, Cheddleton. Tel: 01782
502907. Open Easter–Oct,
daily. Free.
Cheddleton Railway Centre
Cheddleton Station, Churnet
Valley Railway. Tel: 01538
360522. Steam trains operate
Sun and Bank Hol Mon
Easter–Oct, also Wed in Aug.

Diesel trains Sat in Jul and Aug.
Chestnut Centre
Castleton Road, Chapel-en-le-Frith. Tel: 01298 814099. A conservation park, otter haven and owl sanctuary in landscaped grounds. Open Jan–Feb, weekends, Mar–Dec, daily.
Hare Hill
4 miles (6.4km) north of Macclesfield off B5087. Tel: 01625 828981. Parkland with walled garden and pergola. Open end Mar–Oct, most days.
Lyme Park
Disley. Tel: 01663 762023. Open May: Apr–Oct most afternoons; park: all year daily, gardens: Apr–Oct daily.
Macclesfield Silk Museum
Heritage Centre, Roe Street. Tel: 01625 613210. The story of silk and its relevance to Macclesfield is explained, using displays and audio-visual programmes. Open all year, most days.
Paradise Mill
Park Lane, Macclesfield. Tel: 01625 618228. This was a working silk mill until 1981, some of the looms have been restored and the story of silk production is narrated by guides. There are also demonstrations by weavers. Open all year, most afternoons.
Pavilion Gardens
Buxton. Tel: 01298 23114. Gardens, miniature railway and lake. Open all year. Free.
Poole's Cavern
Green Lane, Buxton. Tel: 01298 26978. Open Mar–Oct.
West Park Museum
West Park, Prestbury Road, Macclesfield. Tel: 01625 619831. Local history, paintings by the bird artist Charles Tunnicliffe and a small collection of Egyptian antiquities. Open all year, most afternoons.

SPECIAL INTEREST FOR CHILDREN

The following places may be of interest to visitors with children. Unless otherwise stated, there will be an admission charge.
Blackbrook – The Zoological Park of the Moorlands
Wink Hill, near Leek. Tel: 01538

308293. Many species of birds, as well as a children's farm and pets' area, with pygmy goats, donkeys and rabbits. Open Easter–Oct daily .
Cheddleton Railway Centre
Cheddleton Station, Churnet Valley Railway. Tel: 01538 360522. Steam trains operate Sun and Bank Hol Mon Easter–Oct, also Wed in Aug. Diesel trains Sat in Jul and Aug. Santa steam in Dec.
Chestnut Centre
Castleton Road, Chapel-en-le-Frith. Tel: 01298 814099. A conservation park, otter haven and owl sanctuary. Open Jan–Feb, weekends, Mar–Dec, daily.

Shopping

Buxton
Market Tue and Sat.
Chapel-en-le-Frith
Market Thu.
Leek
General market Wed; general, antiques and bric-à-brac, Sat. The town is a centre for silk and embroidery.
Macclesfield
Outdoor market Tue, Fri, Sat.

LOCAL SPECIALITIES

Water
Spa water flows from the fountain in The Crescent, Buxton. Peak District Bottled Water and Buxton Mineral Water available everywhere.
Patés and sausages
Connoisseurs Supplies Ltd, Elysee House, Harpur Hill, Buxton.
Homemade Charcuterie and Patisserie
Pugson's of Buxton, Cliff House, Terrace Road, Buxton.

The Performing Arts

Buxton
Buxton Opera House, Water Street, Buxton. Tel: 01298 72190.

Sports, Activities and the Outdoors

ANGLING

Fly
Marton Heath Trout Pools, Pike Low Farm, School Lane, Marton, Macclesfield. Tel: 01260 300389.
Tittesworth Reservoir. Tel: 01538 300389.
Coarse
Biddulph Grange Country Park, Grange Road, Biddulph, Stoke-on-Trent. Tel: 01782 522447.
Marton Heath Trout Pools, Pike Low Farm, School Lane, Marton, Macclesfield. Tel: 01260 224231.
Rudyard Lake. Tel: 01538 306280.

BOAT HIRE

Rudyard Lake
Tel: 01538 33280.
Tittesworth Reservoir
Tel: 01538 300400.

COUNTRY PARKS AND NATURE RESERVES

Grinlow and Buxton Country Park.
Tittesworth Reservoir and Visitor Centre. Off A53 Leek–Buxton road, Tel: 01538 300224. Bird hide and nature trail. Open all year except Christmas Day.

Resting under the trees on the tranquil Peak Forest Canal

CYCLING

The Middlewood Way
Runs northwards from Macclesfield.

CYCLE HIRE

Bollington
Groundwork Macclesfield and Vale Royal, Adelphi Mill Gate Lodge, Grimshaw Lane, Bollington, Macclesfield, Cheshire.
Tel: 01625 572681.

Parsley Hey
Parsley Hey Bike Hire.
Tel: 01298 84493.

Whaley Bridge
The Bike Factory, 3 Market Street. Tel: 01663 735020.

GOLF COURSES

Buxton
Cavendish Golf Club, Gadley Lane. Tel: 01298 25052.

Chapel-en-le-Frith
Chapel-en-le-Frith Golf Club, The Cockyard, Manchester Road. Tel: 01298 812118.

Leek
Leek Golf Club, Birchall.
Tel: 01538 385889/384767.
Westwood, Wallbridge, Newcastle Road. Tel: 01538 398385.

Macclesfield
Macclesfield Golf Club, The Hollins. Tel: 01625 615845/423227.

Poynton
Davenport Golf Club, Worth Hall, Middlewood Road.
Tel: 01625 876951.

Town End
Buxton and High Peak Golf Club. Tel: 01298 23453.

GOLF DRIVING RANGE

Adlington
Adlington Golf Centre, Sandy Hey Farm. Tel: 01625 850660.

GUIDED WALKS

Professional Blue Badge Guides can arrange walks for indiviuals or for parties. Tel: 01629 534284.

Buxton
Guided walks, for which a charge is made, start at the Tourist Information Centre and last for approximately 1½ hours. Jun–Sep.

Crag Pass
Walks to packhorse bridge, trails into Dene Valley where three counties meet.
For more details contact Buxton Tourist Information Centre.

Etherow–Goyt Walks
For more information contact the Warden, Etherow Country Park. Tel: 0161 4276937.

Walking the Bollin Valley
For more information contact the Bollin Valley Project Office.
Tel: 01625 534790.

Walks with a Ranger
For a full programme contact Peak District National Park 24-hour information line Tel: 01629 816327.

HANG-GLIDING

Leek
Peak Hang Gliding School, York House, Ladderedge, Leek.
Tel: 01538 382520.

HORSE-RIDING

Flash
North Field Riding & Trekking Centre, Flash.
Tel: 01298 22543.

LONG-DISTANCE FOOTPATHS AND TRAILS

The Brindley Trail
The Brindley Trail runs for 61 miles (98.2km) from Buxton to Stoke-on-Trent.

The Gritstone Trail
The Gritstone Trail runs for 18 miles (29km) from Lyme Park in Cheshire to Rushton Spencer in Staffordshire, where it joins the Staffordshire Way. For more information contact Cheshire County Council. Tel: 01244 602424.

The Middlewood Way
The Middlewood Way runs north from Macclesfield.

The Monsal Trail
Runs for 8½ miles (13.7km) from Blackwell Mill Junction near Buxton to Coombs Viaduct near Bakewell.

The Staffordshire Way
This runs for 92 miles (148km) from Mow Cop to Kinver Edge.

ROCK-CLIMBING

Buxton
Whitehall Open Country

Pursuits, Long Hill.
Tel: 01298 23260.

SAILING

Macclesfield Canal
Lyme View Marina Tel: 01625 874638.

Stanley Reservoir
North Staffordshire Sailing Club Tel: 01782 504240.

Annual Events and Customs

Buxton
Antiques Fair, early/mid-May.
Well-dressing demonstration, early July.
Well-dressing, mid-July.
Buxton Opera Festival mid to late July.
International Arts Festival, mid-July/August.
Buxton Jazz Festival, late July.
International Gilbert & Sullivan Festival, late July/early August.
Country Music Festival, early September.

Cheddleton
Carnival, early August.

Leek
Leek Extravaganza, held every two years, late May.
Leek Arts Festival, late April–end May.

Macclesfield
Sheep Dog Trials, early August.

Macclesfield Forest
Rush-bearing ceremony, St Stephen's Church, early August.

The checklists give details of just some of the facilities covered by the area within this guide. Further information can be obtained from the local Tourist Information Centres.

The White Peak

Bakewell is the mid-point of the Peak District and through it flows
the Wye. The town is the only major settlement for
miles; downstream are willow trees and
broad meadows, and the finest medieval
mansion in all England, Haddon Hall.
Upstream the pace of the river quickens as
the valley narrows; on all sides are hills, a
solid table-top of pale grey limestone. Side-
valleys twist and elbow their way through the
fossil seabed; some carry streams, others are dry as bone. Water often
flows far below the ground, so that in past centuries villages relied on wells,
and gave thanks each summer for their constancy. The White Peak is a land
of drystone walls and beautiful dales, of crouched churches and good pubs,
of sharp winds and bright sunshine.

ASHFORD IN THE WATER Derbyshire Map ref SK1969

Only 2 miles (3.2km) from Bakewell and just off the
busy A6, it is a wonder that Ashford has kept any kind
of dignity. In fact it is one of the most attractive and
interesting of all the Peak villages, sited on a twist of the
River Wye, on the ancient Portway but bypassed by the
new road.

*Attractive Ashford in the
Water remains an unspoiled
Derbyshire village*

VIRGIN CROWNS

In Ashford church hang four
18th-century virgin crants or
crowns. These were funeral
garlands, carried at maidens'
funerals and then hung on
beams or from the roof of the
church. They are made of
white paper attached to a
wicker frame, and in the
middle is a paper glove,
bearing the name of the girl.
The tradition of virgin crowns
was widespread across
England, but rarely do any of
the fragile garlands survive to
tell the sad tale.

CANDLE-MAKERS' DREGS
Greaves Lane, bounding the Hall Orchard to the east of the village of Ashford in the Water, probably got its name from the candle factory that operated here. 'Greaves' were the dregs of fibre, skin or hair that were left after the animal fat had been boiled down to make tallow.

Grassland and the A6 have taken the place of the black marble works on the approach to the village. 'Black marble' was an impure limestone which turned shiny black when polished; it was very popular in Victorian times (for vases, fire-surrounds etc) and the works were extensive and probably represented the only blot on the Ashford horizon. This is not to say there had not been industry in the village before Henry Watson established his marble works in 1748. It simply means the scale was different. Many of the wonderful stone houses and cottages on the main triangle of lanes served as workshops when they were built; there was a corn mill, a candle maker and several stocking mills. The community was more varied and the buildings more eccentric, and this has left a distinctive character to the place today, part pretty English village, part quirky Derbyshire jumble.

At the middle of Ashford is a green space, called Hall Orchard, once part of the grounds of Neville Hall, a medieval hunting lodge which stood on the eastern side. The space is now a playing field but there are some tall trees, notably limes, and around the rest of the village there are some fine ash trees to offer shelter and shade. 'Oak won't grow in Ashford' goes the local saying, and this has proved true over the years. On Church Street, between the Hall Orchard and the Wye, stands a 17th-century tithe barn (now a private house) and the parish church. Most of the structure of the church is Victorian but above the porch, returned to its original position, is a Norman tympanum. The Normans were not as good as the Saxons had been at carving animals, and there is some doubt about what the stone slab depicts. It may be a tree of life with a boar on one side and a lion on the other, or it may be meant to represent the Royal Forest with a boar and a wolf.

Feeding the ducks on the River Wye at Ashford

The main attraction for casual visitors to Ashford is the river, crystal clear and full of trout. There is space to wander along the banks, and three bridges, of which two are old. Close to the cricket field the bridge on the closed road carries an inscription 'M. Hyde 1664'; the brief memorial refers to The Reverend Hyde who was thrown from his horse and drowned in the river below. Upstream, on an old packhorse trail, is the attractive Sheepwash Bridge; a stone fold on one side shows where the sheep were held before being plunged into the river and made to swim across to clean their fleeces.

Southwest of Ashford, on the dry limestone plateau, is Sheldon, a small lead-mining village close to the famous Magpie Mine. The main shaft of the mine was 728 feet (222m) deep and water had to be pumped up to a sough, which carried it to the Wye on the curve below Great Shacklow Wood. In 1966 the roof of the sough collapsed and there was an explosion of pent-up mud and rocks. The resulting debris can still be seen today; the floodwater was gone all too quickly in a tidal wave.

Over the years Ashford has grown used to being flooded – 'in the Water' was added to the name quite recently.

Ashford's low, pleasing Victorian church has few pretentions

TROUT WATCHING

One of the idlest pleasures on rivers like the Wye is to stand on a bridge and watch trout keeping station against the current below. Swimming against the flow looks remarkably easy, if you have the fins for it. Brown trout, with spotted flanks, are the native game fish made famous by *The Compleat Angler*; the rainbow trout is an American import, able to tolerate warmer and more polluted water.

An elegant five-arched bridge crosses the Wye at Bakewell

BAKEWELL PUDDINGS
The fame of the Bakewell Pudding has spread far beyond the bounds of Derbyshire to become high on the list of favourite traditional British puddings. According to tradition, the recipe was the result of a mistake which emanated from the kitchen of the Rutland Arms Hotel in around 1860. The cook, flustered perhaps by the order to prepare a special strawberry tart for some important guests, put the jam in first and then poured in the egg mixture designed for the pastry on top. Far from being a disaster, the new invention was hailed as a culinary triumph and became a regular item on the menu.
Incidentally, do not ask for a Bakewell Tart in the home of their origin – they are always known here as 'puddings'. And don't ask who has the original recipe, included in the will of the Rutland Arms cook – it is still the cause of local dispute and rivalry!

BAKEWELL Derbyshire Map ref SK2168

Bakewell is always busy. Its streets are never free of traffic and bustle, but if this is accepted from the outset there is every reason to enjoy the town; it is an exhilarating mixture of old and new, a tourist honeypot that still serves a working community.

Very old buildings are surprisingly few considering the venerable history of Bakewell (it was granted a market and 15-day fair in 1254), but there are several fine 17th-century structures, such as the Market Hall, which now serves as the Peak National Park Information Centre, and the Town Hall. Up the steep road on the west side of the town stands an airy grass-covered knoll on which sits the parish church of All Saints. Like many Derbyshire churches it is broad and low, but with a spire as sharp as a 3H pencil. Inside there are fascinating fragments of Saxon and Norman stonework, and the famous monument to Sir John Manners and his wife Dorothy, who are supposed to have eloped together from Haddon Hall in 1558. Outside stands the shaft of a 9th-century cross, beautifully and obscurely decorated with vine scrolls and figures. Close to the church is Cunningham Place and The Old House, a 16th-century parsonage turned museum.

Monday is market day in Bakewell, when cattle and sheep wagons converge behind Bridge Street and the market place is decked with awnings. Escaping the bleating and banter is easy; the River Wye runs alongside, and it is possible in a few seconds to be out of the crowd and feeding ducks or trout along the river. Upstream is one of the oldest bridges in England, built in about 1300; impossible to appreciate if you are driving over it but a scene-stealer from water level where its five arches and solid breakwaters are visible. In the distance is Castle Hill, where the settlement of Bakewell began in 920 with the establishment of a Mercian fort.

EYAM Derbyshire Map ref SK2176

Disease was a fact of life in medieval England, and many Peakland villages suffered the horrors of black death and plague. What made the weaving village of Eyam special was the attempt by the rector, William Mompesson, to keep the outbreak in 1665–6 within the confines of the community and not let it be carried elsewhere. The whole village was quarantined, entire families perished and Eyam became a byword for tragedy and self-sacrifice.

According to tradition, the plague virus (carried by fleas on black rats) was introduced into the village by a tailor called George Viccars who had bought some infected cloth from London. He died a few days after arriving at Eyam, lodging with Mary Cooper at what is now called Plague Cottage. A fortnight later Mary's son Edward died and the whole community braced itself for disaster. The young rector quickly sent his own children away, but stayed with his wife to care for the sick and organise the quarantine. Over the months, through 1665 and into the autumn of 1666, about 250 people died, including Mompesson's wife, but the heroic efforts of the village were successful and the epidemic did not spread.

Some of the story has been embellished in the telling, but the essential details are recorded in the parish register, among the gravestones around St Lawrence's Church and on nearby cottages. Towns such as Derby and Chesterfield probably suffered worse epidemics of bubonic plague; Eyam has kept its unique place in history because you can stand beside victims' homes, read about their lives and look across to their graves.

Eyam today is neither sad nor dwelling in the past. It stands on the hill brow between Middleton Dale and Eyam Moor, as self-contained and aloof as ever. Visitors are impressed by the fine Saxon cross in St Lawrence's churchyard and come to enjoy the well-dressing and the sheep roast. But folk-memories of the plague still send a shiver down the spine.

GEOLOGY OF THE PLAGUE VILLAGE

Exploring the upper pathways of the village, such as the grassy alley from the Royal Oak up Little Edge and along May Walk, it is obvious that Eyam lies on the very edge of the limestone and only just qualifies as a White Peak village. In fact, most of the houses on the north side, towards Eyam Edge, are made of sandstone which was the preferred building material, whilst the greyer, less durable limestone was used a few hundred yards away to the south. Across the valley, and rarely mentioned in tourist guidebooks, you can see two great working quarries, ripping into the hills for roadstone.

An inscribed chair in Eyam church commemorates William Mompesson, the courageous rector here during the plague of 1665–6

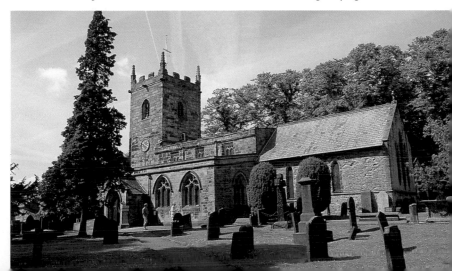

HADDON HALL   Derbyshire Map ref SK2366

Close your eyes and imagine a rambling family castle,
built with style, English to the core, unchanged for
centuries, full of ghosts, set among trees and pastures
above a clear meandering river. What you have in mind
is probably Haddon Hall. It is the single most impressive
and authentic building in the Peak District, the one that
turns historians into poets. Why is this? The simple
explanation is that it is a perfectly proportioned
medieval manor house, hardly touched since the 16th
century. The rest is atmosphere and imagination.

Haddon was owned by the Vernon family from 1170
until 1567; it came to them by marriage and passed to
the Manners family in the same way. Over all those years
the house was extended gradually; the Peveril Tower in
the 12th century, the cross-wing in the 14th,
battlements in the 15th, a gatehouse and courtyard in
the 16th and the Long Gallery early in the 17th. But
after that Haddon Hall was left to slumber while the
Manners family moved to the magnificent Belvoir Castle
as Dukes of Rutland.

Thus the house escaped the architectural fashions of
the 18th and 19th centuries, but it was not neglected – it
was meticulously maintained, so that when the 9th
Duke (then the Marquis of Granby) began his restoration
of Haddon in the early 20th century, his task was by no
means daunting. The Duke ensured that as much as
possible of the original structure should be preserved,
and that any replacements were carried out to the
highest standards. Today Haddon reflects a sense of
history which can only come from remaining in the
same family for over 800 years. Whether Dorothy
Vernon really did escape down the long staircase, out
from the chapel to the packhorse bridge to elope with
John Manners in 1558, is open to question, but perfectly
in keeping with the romance of the place.

*Extravagant topiary
ornaments the gardens at
Haddon Hall*

LATHKILL DALE Derbyshire Map ref SK1867

The classic farmscape of silver-green pastures criss-crossed by drystone walls is dramatically disrupted on the White Peak plateau by the Derbyshire Dales, a series of steep-sided valleys etched into the limestone. The best dales are gathered together to form a National Nature Reserve, and the jewel in the crown is Lathkill Dale which runs eastwards from the village of Monyash to the River Wye below Haddon. Access to Lathkill Dale is from Monyash or Over Haddon, 2 miles (3.2km) southwest of Bakewell.

From the east the dale starts dry but between Ricklow and Cales Dale the River Lathkill rises out of a cave and soon broadens into a beautiful, crystal-clear stream, the haunt of water voles and dippers.

Unlike the pasture and silage fields of the plateau, the grassland of the dale is ablaze with wild flowers. The rabbit-cropped south-facing slopes sparkle with rockrose and trefoil, which attract blue butterflies and burnet and forester moths. The shaded herbage of the north-facing slopes is the habitat for one of the Dales' specialities, Jacob's ladder. Further down the Lathkill, following the well-worn footpath towards Over Haddon, grassland gives way to scrub and to ash woodland which, in the early summer particularly, casts a translucent shade and is full of songbirds.

Lathkill Dale may look untouched, but for many centuries it was mined for lead. The shafts, drainage channels and spoil-heaps have been absorbed into the natural landscape to such an extent that they really enhance its natural beauty. Most of the lead had been exhausted by the 18th century but in the 1840s there was a grandiose attempt to drain the deep mines by building a steam engine, powered by a huge waterwheel fed by the Mandale viaduct. The scheme was a disaster, as was the Over Haddon gold rush of 1894.

A REGULAR REMEDY

One of Lathkill Dale's special tree species is the purging buckthorn. It is the food plant of the brimstone butterfly, but got its name from the medieval use of its berries. Excavations of the latrines of old monasteries have unearthed huge numbers of buckthorn seeds. Clearly, penance for monks was an uncomfortable business.

Lead mining shaped the landscape of lovely Lathkill Dale

*A shady pool with an air of
mystery, Miller's Dale*

MILLER'S DALE   Derbyshire Map ref SK1474

The Wye rises at Buxton but then flows east to dissect
the limestone plateau. Each reach of the river has its
own character, and each section of the narrow valley or
dale has its own name. Thus Wye Dale turns into Chee
Dale, which gives way to Miller's Dale, then Water-cum-
Jolly Dale and Monsal Dale. They are names to conjure
with, to stir the imagination.

The presence of the river is a unifying theme; it
brought industry to the outback in the heady days of the
Industrial Revolution and around this industry the little
settlement of Miller's Dale grew up, squeezed awkwardly
into the narrow valley of the Wye. Here lived the rail
men and quarry workers and their families, and there
was even a station, but all of that is gone now and the
industrial areas are returning to nature.

In many respects Miller's Dale, to either side of Litton
Mill, is the most impressive and complete dale to visit.
Not only does the Wye negotiate a barrage of natural
obstacles here, side-stepping hills, twisting through gaps
and gorges and rock faces, but also there are mill races
and weirs where the power of the water has been
diverted to drive 19th-century cotton mills (Litton and

Cressbrook, a little way downstream). A long-distance footpath, the Monsal Trail, runs the length of the dale allowing access to the old mill yards (some of the buildings are still in use, but not for weaving). There are footbridges at either end of Miller's Dale allowing access to convenient car parks.

Several side dales run north from the main valley, often dry and grassy but sometimes decked with ash woodland and with a stream dancing down to meet the Wye. The most attractive are Cressbrook Dale, the best for wildlife and with some beautiful ash woodland, Tideswell Dale with access to the village of Tideswell (see Walk on page 58), and Monks Dale, close to the village of Wormhill. Wormhill belies its name by being an attractive scatter of old farmhouses, with a village green, stocks and a fountain/well (dressed in August) commemorating James Brindley, the famous canal engineer, who was born close by at Tunstead.

The Monsal Trail long-distance footpath runs the length of the valley

DIPPERS IN MILLER'S DALE
The most characteristic bird of White Peak rivers is the dipper, the shape of a wren, but ten times the size and with a pure white breast. Dippers feed on small fish and aquatic insects, for which they dive or wade, using their half-open wings against the current to keep them submerged.

Litton and the Dales

Meltwater under the ice caps scooped out the dales and left a network of valleys through which rivers could flow. This walk links a litany of dales, some with wooded slopes and pretty streams, others dry with rock tors and terraces of flowers. Six in all, rejoicing in such names as Cressbrook and Water-cum-Jolly.

Time: 4 hours. Distance: 6 miles (9.7km).
Location: 1 mile (1.6km) south of Tideswell.
Start: Drive south from Tideswell village on the B6049. Park at the Peak National Park picnic site at Tideswell Dale.
(OS Grid ref: SK154742.)
OS Map: Outdoor Leisure 24
(The Peak District – White Peak area) 1:25,000.
See Key to Walks on page 121.

ROUTE DIRECTIONS

Leave the car park on the broad path from the toilet block down the dale. Ignore a fork left shortly after the first gate, signed 'Picnic Area'. From a footbridge there is a choice of paths on either side of a stream – they come back together at another bridge. Keep on down the dale beside the stream. **Ravenstor**, now

Look for the curious Chimney Cottage at Litton Mill

a youth hostel, is perched on a crag ahead on the right.

Join a tarmac road at the bottom of the dale. Bear left along it to **Litton Mill** and go through the gateway into the Mill Yard. At the end of the mill buildings cross a bridge right over the mill race and follow the Monsal Trail downstream, alongside the Wye through **Miller's Dale and Water-cum-Jolly Dale**.

Keep on the left bank, cross a footbridge and bear left, around the extensive site of **Cressbrook Mill**, turn left on to a tarmac road and turn immediately right when the road forks. Walk uphill for about a quarter of a mile (0.4km) then fork right down to Ravensdale Cottages. The path passes to the left of the cottages and follows the stream. Ignore a rising path to the left. At a footbridge enter **Cressbrook Dale**. Shortly afterwards bear right at a fork. The path now climbs away from the stream and out of the trees into open country. When a corner of a wall is reached, bear left downhill back to the valley floor.

Cross the stream via the stepping stones and head for the cleft ahead which is Tansley Dale. When you see a wall ahead the path bears right to a stile; after this bear right to the corner of a wall. Continue ahead to a stile by a gate and turn left along a walled lane for a few yards. Cross over a stile to the right then head diagonally across to the far left corner of the field, over another stile and on to a road.

Turn left to Litton village green. Walk through the village, bear left at the Red Lion and go downhill through Litton Dale. Bear left at a T-junction to walk down Tideswell Dale and return to the picnic site.

POINTS OF INTEREST

Ravenstor
Many placenames in the area relate to the ravens which once nested on the dales' crags but disappeared over a century ago. Ravens have recently returned to Derbyshire but are very elusive; it is their smaller relatives, the jackdaws, which are often seen in noisy gaggles around the quarries and crags.

Litton Mill

The success of textile mills in the early years of the 19th century was based on cheap power and a ready supply of labour. The power came from the river, whilst children, often orphans, were used as labour. Cruelty and exploitation were universal, but Litton Mill earned an especially evil reputation. Many children died of disease and beatings and were buried secretly in unmarked graves.

Miller's Dale and Water-cum-Jolly Dale

The dramatic limestone gorge twists and turns as the Wye flows westwards. In summer dippers and grey wagtails are often seen close together on the river. They could hardly look less alike, the dipper stubby and brown with a white bib, the grey wagtail slim and graceful with a very long tail, blue-grey back and sulphur-yellow breast.

Cressbrook Mill

William Newton, manager of this 19th-century cotton mill in its heyday, gained a reputation for treating his workers well, although eyewitness accounts suggest he was no better, or worse, than anyone else.

Cressbrook Dale

Part of the Derbyshire Dales National Nature Reserve, and especially important for limestone flowers. Yellow Star of Bethlehem, Nottingham Catchfly and Bloody Cranesbill are among the species found here. Ravencliffe Cave was used by prehistoric hunters, following herds of wild cattle and reindeer in interglacial times.

Litton

There are pretty stone cottages from the days of the lead-mining boom, and the village green has a pair of stocks.

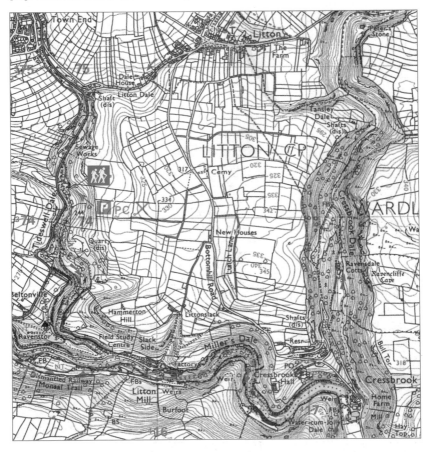

PEAK FOREST WEDDINGS
Because Peak Forest church was on Crown land, not in the jurisdiction of a bishop, the village priest was able to grant marriage licences and the place gained a reputation as an 18th-century Gretna Green. An Act of Parliament put paid to this romantic and lucrative business. The present church building dates back to Victorian times: the original structure was to the east, on the far side of the graveyard. Some of its stonework, and a window, were used for the village reading room.

PEAK FOREST Derbyshire Map ref SK1179

High, wide and windswept, it is hard to believe that this landscape of sheep pasture was once a royal chase, the Forest in the Peak, or that its administrative capital was this little village. For about a century, until the relaxation of the Forest Laws in 1250, kings and princes used the vast expanse of woodland and heath between the Rivers Goyt and the Derwent as a private playground; they hunted wild boar and roe deer and stayed at the recently built Peveril Castle which stands high above Castleton to the northeast.

By Elizabethan times most of the ancient woodland had disappeared, but what remained of the wilderness was fenced in as a deer park, which extended to about four square miles. A Steward and five Royal Foresters managed the enclosure system and had premises in the Chamber, a building on the site of the present Chamber Farm. Swainmotes, or forest courts, settled any disputes. It was the foresters' task to care for the deer, by controlling grazing in the areas of pasture, by preventing walls from being built and by keeping people out. The deer increased four-fold, but this was only a temporary triumph. Around 1655 the land was allocated to the Dukes of Devonshire and was officially deforested, though in fact the last of the trees had already been felled to provide pit props for the coal mines on Coombs Moss. Scrub and heath took over the countryside until the turn of the 19th century.

The village of Peak Forest is set in rolling pastureland

The Chamber of the Peak, and the few cottages that made up the village of Peak Forest, had been the heart of the royal forest, but had not stood among trees; this part of the limestone plateau was called the Great Pasture and was used for sheep, as it is now. The present village of stone-built houses and farms grew up around a church built by the Dowager Duchess of Devonshire when the land was first acquired. This was at the time of the Commonwealth and could only be construed as an act of defiance, particularly considering its dedication – to 'King Charles, King and Martyr'.

Considering its colourful past, Peak Forest is a modest little place. A post office and pub (The Devonshire Arms of course) cater for any secular needs.

STANTON IN PEAK Derbyshire Map ref SK2364
Ritual landscapes, stretches of countryside set aside in prehistoric times because of their spiritual significance, are not confined to Stonehenge and the Dorset Cercus. Apart from megaliths and barrows, such places often retain traces of avenues and earth banks, dykes and cairns. They draw the eye from miles around, dominating the high ground and casting a powerful spell, on everyone from archaeologists to New Age travellers. They ask so many questions of our modern culture that they are as uncomfortable as they are fascinating. Such a place is Stanton Moor.

An old cairn on Stanton Moor marks an earlier civilisation

WYE VALLEY VIEWPOINT
Pilhough Lane, going northeast out of Stanton, makes a pleasant walk or drive because of its superb views over the Wye Valley and Haddon Hall. Before the church was built parishioners had to walk this way to Rowsley, and the Thornhill family had a viewing platform, called the Belvedere or Stand, set into the steep edge so that people could rest and enjoy the prospect.

ROCKING STONES

Many of the sandstone outcrops that rise out of the tide of bracken between Stanton and Elton have historical associations. Rowtor Rocks, near Birchover and overlooking the Druid Inn, was famous for its Rocking Stones, but the best of these, a 50-ton block wobbling on a sandstone pivot, was vandalised in 1799 and will no longer move. At the foot of nearby Cratcliff Rocks is a hermit's cave, once the abode of a rabbit-catcher.

The oddly blocked windows of Holly House at Stanton in Peak may have been filled in to avoid a punitive window tax

Stanton village is a ribbon of cottages on a steep and winding side road, out of the limestone and below the brow of the gritstone, sheltered from the moor by old quarries and a swathe of tall sweet-chestnut trees. The initials WPT, carved into the lintels of many doorways, refer to William Thornhill, who built most of the village in the 1830s and whose family lived at Stanton Hall. The Flying Childers Inn dates back to the 18th century and celebrates the greatest racehorse of its day, trained by Sir Hugh Childers for the 4th Duke of Devonshire. Opposite the inn stands Holly House, with half of its windows still blocked up to avoid the window tax of 1697.

Birchover Lane, running south of Stanton, follows the western edge of the moor. Parking places give access to pathways through birch scrub and over heather and bilberry to the Bronze-Age landscape. About 70 barrows or burial cairns have been identified on the small island of gritstone; many have been excavated but the majority have not. The biggest, covering the site of twelve cremations, still stands at 5 feet (1.5m) tall, in a double ring of stones with an outer diameter of 54 feet (16.4m). There are three stone circles or monuments on Stanton Moor, the most famous is known as the Nine Ladies. Outside this ring of stones, about 100 feet (30.5m) to the south, stands the solitary King Stone, which is certainly part of the ritual site. The story goes that a fiddler and nine maidens were turned to stone for dancing on Sunday. In such ways prehistoric culture was trivialised.

TIDESWELL Derbyshire Map ref SK1575

Daniel Defoe, searching for the famous 'Seven Wonders of the Peak' in the 1720s, was not impressed by the ebbing and flowing well in a garden of Manchester Road in Tideswell. This may have been because he was looking at the wrong well (the original 'Wonder' was probably at Barmoor Clough), but in any case the water no longer ebbs and flows with the tide, and Tideswell got its name from an ancient British chieftain called Tidi! This is not to say that wells were not important in the village; it lies at the 1,000-foot contour on the limestone plateau, set in a dry bowl amid a grey cobwebbing of walls and wind-scorched fields. In fact Tideswell is renowned for the quality of its well-dressing ceremony, which starts the Wakes Week on the Saturday nearest John the Baptist's Day (24 June); the week's festivities are concluded with a torchlight procession and a unique Morris Dance.

TIDESWELL CROSSES

In the 15th century all the roads around Tideswell were marked by stone crosses. Only one of these survives intact, at Wheston to the west, close to the 17th-century hall; the rest exist in fragments, their water-filled bases built into walls and gateposts. A local tradition is to float a cross made of grass blades on to the water and make a wish.

The soaring Perpendicular tower of Tideswell church, with its unusual eight-pinnacled top

The steep-sided valley of Cressbrook Dale lies to the southeast of Tideswell

THE SEVEN WONDERS OF THE PEAK

The 'Seven Wonders of the Peak' first appeared in print in 1622 in a set of poems by Michael Drayton. His list included Peak Cavern, Poole's Cavern, Eldon Hole, St Ann's Well, the ebbing and flowing well at Tideswell, Mam Tor and Peak Forest. Some years later Thomas Hobbes wrote a poem also including Seven Wonders, but substituting Chatsworth House for Peak Forest. It was left to the redoubtable traveller, Daniel Defoe, in his Tour of 1726, to debunk the myth of the wonders – including the singularly unimpressive well at Tideswell.

In the 14th century Tideswell was a thriving place, confident in the future of the wool trade and lead mining. The parish church, dedicated to John the Baptist, reflected this optimism; it was built in just 75 years and was a classic cruciform shape, of Decorated and Perpendicular styles, spacious and with superb fittings, carvings and brasses. That Tideswell dwindled to a village was in some ways a stroke of luck, particularly in that the glorious church, often described as the 'Cathedral of the Peak', was bypassed by rich patrons and Victorian megalomaniacs, and stands today in splendid unaltered isolation. Around it run lawns and railings separating it from the more prosaic buildings at the heart of the village.

Two of Tideswell's musical forefathers are buried in the church: 'the Minstrel of the Peak', William Newton, who died in 1830, and Samuel Slack, who died in 1822. Slack, whose name bore no relation to his vocal chords, was famous for two things: singing for George III and for stopping a bull dead in its tracks by bellowing at it. His voice, apparently, could be heard a mile away.

To the east of Tideswell is the little village of Litton, a pretty gathering of 18th-century cottages beside a green with a set of stocks close to the Red Lion pub. Tideswell Dale and Cressbrook Dale run south, from west and east of the village, beautiful in their own right and giving access to dramatic Miller's Dale.

WINSTER Derbyshire Map ref SK2460

Midway between the sleepy little villages of Elton and
Wensley (which has its own Wensley Dale, but without
the cheese) rests the sleepy little village of Winster.
People go to Winster because they intend to; it lies off
the main tourist routes, though close enough to Matlock
to make use of its shops and services. Most of the
attraction of the village is its character, as an old lead-
mining centre with 18th-century houses lining the main
street between a 17th-century Dower House and a 15th-
to 16th-century Market House. The latter is matchbox-
sized, a delightful structure of weathered stone arches,
once open but now bricked in to keep it all standing,
and an upper floor of brick, which may have replaced an
earlier timbered affair. The Market House was bought by
the National Trust in 1906, its first acquisition in the
Peak District, and part of it is now used as an
Information Centre. Close by is Winster Hall, an early
Georgian house, now a hotel and said to be haunted.

Winster used to be full of alehouses; witness the name
Shoulder of Mutton, carved by the door of what is now a
private house on West Bank. At the top of the bank, just
out of the village, is the still-thriving Miners Standard,
which has on display some of the old lead-mining
equipment. It is here that the traditional Winster Morris
perform their dances at the start of Wakes Week in June
each year; a procession then leads through the village,
finishing up at the Miners Standard for refreshment. A
more recent, less obviously pagan, tradition is that of
pancake-racing on Shrove Tuesday. It began as harmless
fun, organised by the local headmaster as a wartime
diversion for the children, but is now a seriously light-
hearted affair, with secret training and stringent rules
about the batter.

WINSTER'S MUSICAL HERITAGE

'Blue-eyed Stranger' and 'The
Winster Gallop' are two of the
best-known Morris tunes in
the country, played wherever
the Cotswold tradition of
Morris Dancing is followed.
But their home is Winster. At
the turn of the 20th century
the tunes were 'collected' by
the legendary Cecil Sharpe
and were then rediscovered in
the folk revival of the 1960s
and 70s.

*The Miners' Standard inn,
just outside Winster, is still a
popular focus for local
activities*

Youlgreave's circular water tank, christened The Fountain, once supplied the whole village

ARBOR LOW'S ANCIENT STONES

Three miles (4.8km) along the Long Rake west of Youlgreave, off the road to the right and accessible from a car park, is the famous henge of Arbor Low, thought to have been built by the Beaker People in around 2,000 BC. The whole monument, with rock-cut ditch, bank and a circle of 47 stones, measures 250 feet (76.2m) across. Although the massive stone blocks are all lying flat and half buried, Arbor Low is still a powerful place, especially in winter sunlight.

YOULGREAVE Derbyshire Map ref SK2064

A long, handsome village on the shoulder of Bradford Dale, Youlgreave (known as Pommie by most locals) has one of the best well-dressing ceremonies in the Peak District, taking place at Midsummer each year, when five wells are dressed with biblical scenes. The White Peak tradition has its roots in the days when wells were essential and were blessed to give thanks for water. However, in the case of Youlgreave the records only go back to 1829, coinciding with the provision of the village's own public water supply via a conduit from the Dale below. The water was gathered in a huge circular stone tank called The Fountain, which stands to this day in the middle of the village. Near by, on the opposite side of the street, is the Co-op building, which once had a vital role in the social survival of the area but is now a youth hostel.

On the east side of Youlgreave, nudging the road which then sweeps down to Alport, stands All Saints Church, described by experts as one of the most impressive churches in Derbyshire. Essentially Norman and with an unusually broad nave, the most obvious feature of All Saints is its 14th-century tower, chunky and stylish in the best Perpendicular tradition. Inside it has sturdy columns and a 13th-century font, unique in that it has two bowls, and the fine monuments include a tiny effigy of Thomas Cokayne, who died in 1488. The church was restored in 1870 and has stained-glass windows by Burne-Jones and Kempe.

Three bridges cross the River Bradford below Youlgreave, including a clapper bridge of stone slabs and a packhorse bridge, now used as a footbridge. The short walk to the confluence with the Lathkill is popular, but by turning southeast, over the main bridge and on to the Limestone Way, it is possible to explore the fine rolling countryside towards Birchover, past the Iron-Age hill-fort of Castle Hill and the Nine Rings Stone Circle (four stones are still standing tall), to the great tumbling rock tors of Robin Hood's Stride (once known as Mock Beggars Hall), Cratcliffe Rocks and Rowtor Rocks. Pagan myths, hermits' caves and a popular little pub, the Druid's Inn, are among the attractions of this magical corner of the Peak.

DEW PONDS

Dew ponds are a feature of limestone pastures in the White Peak. Because the underlying rock is porous there are no natural pools, so farmers have created their own. Nothing to do with dew, the ponds are named after a famous pond-maker, Mr Dew.

Youlgreave, lying south of Bakewell, boasts a fine Norman and later church

The White Peak

Checklist

Leisure Information

Places of Interest

Shopping

Sports, Activities
and the Outdoors

Annual Events and Customs

Leisure Information

TOURIST INFORMATION CENTRE

Bakewell
The Old Market Hall, Bridge Street. Tel: 01629 813227. (Seasonal)

NATIONAL PARK INFORMATION

Peak District National Park
Head Office, Aldern House, Baslow Road, Bakewell. Tel: 01629 816200. www.peakdistrict.org.uk

OTHER INFORMATION

Derbyshire Wildlife Trust
Elvaston Castle, Derby. Tel: 01332 756610.
English Heritage
Canada House, 3 Chepstow Street, Manchester. Tel: 0161 242 1400.
www. english-heritage.org.uk
English Nature
Manor Barn, Over Haddon, Bakewell. Tel: 01629 815095.
National Trust
East Midlands Regional Office, Clumber Park Stableyard, Worksop, Nottinghamshire. Tel: 01909 486411.
Longshaw Estate Office. Tel: 01433 670368.
www.nationaltrust.org.uk

Public Transport
The 'Derbyshire Wayfarer' allows one day's unlimited travel on all local buses and trains in the county. Details from Derbyshire County Council, Public Transport Dept. Tel: 01629 580000.
Derbyshire Busline Tel: 01298 23098.
GMPTE Tel: 0161 288 7811.
South Yorkshire Travelline Tel: 01709 515151.
Rail information Tel: 0345 484950.
www.derbysbus.net
Severn Trent Water
2297 Coventry Road, Birmingham. Tel: 0121 722 4968.
Weather Call
Tel: 0906 850 04187.

ORDNANCE SURVEY MAPS

Landranger 1:50,000 Sheet 119.
Outdoor Leisure 1:25,000 Sheets 1, 24.

Places of Interest

There will be an admission charge at the following places of interest unless otherwise stated.
Arbor Low Stone Circle
Upper Oldhams Farm, Monyash. Open all year, at any reasonable time. Free.

Eyam Hall
Tel: 01433 631976. The furniture, portraits and other items at the Hall reflect the fact that this is still a family home and has been for centuries. Craft centre. Open Apr–Oct limited opening.
Eyam Museum
Tel: 01433 631371. Museum tells the story of the bubonic plague, how it reached Eyam and was contained there. Open Apr–Oct daily except Mon.
Haddon Hall
Bakewell. Tel: 01629 812855. A splendid house that has remained virtually untouched by the passage of time. Open Apr–Sep, daily; Oct Mon–Thu.
Old House Museum
Bakewell. Tel: 01629 813165. This Tudor house is home to a folk museum and a Victorian kitchen; toys and lace are among the exhibits. Open Apr–Oct, afternoons only, daily Jul–Aug.
Winster Market House
Winster, 4 miles (6.4km) west of Matlock. Tel: 01909 486411. Restored by the National Trust, the Market House is now used as an information centre. The buildings dates back to the late 17th/early 18th century. Open Apr–Oct. Free.

Shopping

Bakewell
Market on Mon, includes cattle, except Bank Hol Mons when a general market is held.

LOCAL SPECIALITIES

Bakewell Puddings
Original Bakewell Pudding Shop, The Square, Bakewell.
Tel: 01629 812193.
Bloomers Original Bakewell Puddings, Water Lane, Bakewell.
Tel: 01629 814844.

General Foodstuff
Foods From The Chatsworth Estate, Chatsworth Farm Shop, Stud Farm, Pilsley, Bakewell.
Tel: 01246 583392.
Pork Pies
Connoisseurs Deli, Water Street, Water Lane, Bakewell.
Tel: 01629 814844.

Landscape Photography
Bridget Flemming, Edensor, Bakewell. Peak District landscape photography. Commissions welcome. Tel: 01246 583315.

Stained Glass
Dave Griffin, Bakewell. Designer and maker of high quality stained glass. Commissions welcome. Tel: 01629 814770.

Sports, Activities and the Outdoors

GOLF COURSES

Bakewell
Bakewell Golf Club, Station Road. Tel: 01629 812307.

GUIDED WALKS

Bakewell
Professional Blue Badge Guides can arrange walks for indiviuals or for parties. Tel: 01629 534284.

Derbyshire Dales Countryside Service
Planning and Development Services, Town Hall, Matlock. Full guided walks service. Tel: 01629 761100 for details.

Lathkill Dale
The walks from Lathkill Information Centre, and other start points, are led by an experienced guide and explore the nature reserve. Free. Booking is advisable. Tel: 01298 815095.

National Park Walks with a Ranger
For more details contact the Peak District National Park 24-hour information line Tel: 01629 816327.

LONG-DISTANCE FOOTPATHS AND TRAILS

Bakewell Circular Walk
This is a figure-of-eight route making two 50-mile (80-km) circular walks through the Peak National Park starting and finishing in Bakewell.

The Monsal Trail
This runs for 8½ miles (13.7km) from Blackwell Mill Junction near Buxton to Coombs Viaduct near Bakewell.

Annual Events and Customs

Ashford in the Water
Well-dressing mid-June. Blessing of the Wells Trinity Sunday, May.
Bakewell
Well-dressing, late June/early July.
Carnival, early July.
Bakewell Show, early August.
Eyam
Well-dressing and demonstration late August.
Plague Commemoration Service, September.
Carnival, August/September.
Litton
Well-dressing demonstration, late June. Well-dressing, late June/early July.
Litton Horticultural Show, early September.

Middleton by Youlgreave
Well-dressing demonstration, late May. Well-dressing, late May/early June.
Monyash
Well-dressing demonstration, late May. Well-dressing, late May/early June.
Monyash Antiques and Collectors' Fair, late August.
Pilsley
Well-dressing, mid- to late July.
Stoney Middleton
Well-dressing, late July.
Tideswell
Wakes Week, late June. Well-dressing, late June/early July.
Male Voice Choir and Silver Band Annual Concert, early July.
Winster
Pancake racing, Shrove Tuesday.
Winster Wakes Festivities, late June–early July.
Wormhill
Well-dressing demonstration, late August.
Youlgreave
Well-dressing, late June.

The checklists give details of just some of the facilities covered by the area within this guide. Further information can be obtained from Tourist Information Centres.

Discover the local delicacies in Bakewell

The Derwent Valley and The Eastern Moors

A ribbon of high gritstone moorland runs all the way from Stocksbridge to Matlock, acting as a buffer between the industries and suburbs of Sheffield and Chesterfield and the main artery of the Peak District, the River Derwent. This empty and elemental landscape was deserted by humans when the climate changed in the late Bronze Age and is now the domain of grouse and merlin.

At the edge of the heather moors are great shelves of gritstone, etched by ice into a famous series of west-facing cliffs or Edges, worked for millstones which still litter the birchwoods at their feet. At the head of the Derwent are the dams, holding back the waters of Ladybower. Downstream there are attractive villages, all quite different, and several historic houses, of which Chatsworth stands supreme.

A TEST OF YOUTH

On the brow of Baslow Edge stands the Eagle Stone, a great weathered block of hardened gritstone; climbing to the top of the stone used to be a test of character for village youths before they married. Not far away is the Wellington Monument, erected in 1866 by Dr Wrench, who sounds like a character out of a Dickens novel and was also responsible for the replacement of the numerals on the face of St Anne's Church clock with 'Victoria 1897'.

The massive form of the Eagle Stone, near Baslow

BASLOW Derbyshire Map ref SK2572

The 18th-century turnpike road from Sheffield used to cross the Derwent next to St Anne's Church in the oldest part of Baslow, called Bridge End. A new bridge now spans the river a short distance to the south, making it possible to idle about the 17th-century triple-arched bridge and take a close look at the little toll house (the doorway is just 3½ feet high) that guards it. Further along the lane on the west bank of the river stands Bubnell Hall, which is as old as the bridge, whilst on the east bank, above the main road, stands Baslow Hall, which is a turn-of-the-century copy and has now been converted into the luxurious Fischer's Hotel.

On the far side of Baslow is Nether End, almost a village in itself, gathered around its own little Goose Green and with a row of thatched cottages overlooking Bar Brook. Thatched cottages are now rare in the Peak District, though 'black thatch' (heather or turf) may once have been more widespread. Nether End marks the north entrance to the Chatsworth Estate and there is a touch of class or comfort about everything; this applies equally to the nearby Cavendish Hotel, which contains some fine antiques from Chatsworth House.

Further east along the Sheffield road the Bar Brook cuts a nick in the dramatic gritstone scarp, with Baslow Edge on one side and Birchen Edge on the other. A sea of bracken laps the footings of the rock faces, whilst the moorland above the edge is a wilderness of heather and the home of merlin and grouse. It was once the home of farmers too, in the Bronze Age when the climate was a little kinder. It is astonishing to find field systems still visible from more than 3,000 years ago. Below Baslow Bar, just out of Nether End, it is also possible to see narrow fields separated by drystone walls that follow the old reverse-S pattern, the sign of ox-ploughing in medieval times.

THE DAYLIGHT MOTH
Moths don't always fly at night. On sunny days in the middle of the summer, a little moth called the chimney-sweeper, sooty-black with white fringes, appears along meadow verges, searching for its foodplant, the pignut.

Thatched cottages in a lovely setting by the Bar Brook at Nether End, Baslow

The Snow Road

This tour begins at Baslow, in a cleft of the Derwent valley with gritstone cliffs to the east and the White Peak to the west. It heads north to Ladybower Reservoir, then climbs steadily northwest to cross the Dark Peak by the famous Snake Pass, then drops down to Glossop and Chapel-en-le-Frith. The return route is over the limestone plateau of the White Peak and down-dale through Stoney Middleton. Treat the Snake with caution if there is a hint of snow in the air.

ROUTE DIRECTIONS

See Key to Car Tours on page 120.

The tour starts in Baslow at the roundabout junction of the A619 and the A623 and goes north along the A623 for 1½ miles (2.4km) to Calver. Here continue to the traffic lights and turn right, following the A625, then soon the B6001, signed 'Grindleford', for 2 miles (3.2km), into the little railway town of Grindleford. Turn right on the B6521 and cross the river bridge up into Nether Padley. Continue for 2 miles (3.2km); moss-draped boulders and oak woodland soon give way to open moorland as the road passes the blackened cluster of buildings on the right that is Longshaw Lodge and sweeps up to a T-junction. Turn left, following the A6187 signed for Hathersage. The road then bears left and there are fine views of Hathersage Moor. Discarded millstones lie among the birches, close to where they were cut – look for one in a car park on the right. Drop down off the moor for 3½ miles (5.6km) into the village of Hathersage. The churchyard (on the right up School Lane and Church Bank) boasts the grave of Little John.

Drive through Hathersage, then continue along the A6187 for another mile (1.6km) towards Bamford before turning right opposite the Marquis of Granby Hotel on to the A6013, signed for Bamford and Ladybower. Continue for 2 miles (3.2km), past the dam wall of Ladybower Reservoir, to a T-junction and turn left on the A57, signed for Glossop. Keep to this road for 14 miles (22.5km); it winds up Woodlands Valley, along the length of Ladybower, then up past the Snake Inn.

This is one of the most exposed and lonely places in England, and the road really does snake its way over the dome of moorland before descending to the little mill

Woodlands Valley leads on to the remote Snake Pass

town of Glossop. Head into the town centre and turn left on to the A624, signed 'Chapel-en-le-Frith'. The road now rises on to open country again. Continue for 4 miles (6.4km) to Little Hayfield, then on to Hayfield, with the village on the left and the start of the Sett Valley Trail on the right. Continue on the A624 for 2 miles (3.2km), past the Lamb Inn, with an imposing sweep of green hills and gritstone walls to the left and a hint of industry, New Mills and the Lancashire/Cheshire border, away to the right.

In another mile (1.6km) the road drops under a railway bridge to a junction, where you turn left, following the signs for Chapel-en-le-Frith.

Go under the viaduct at Chapel Milton and into Chapel-en-le-Frith, and at a roundabout continue straight on, still following the signs for Chapel-en-le-Frith. Bear left at a junction following the signs for the A6 to Buxton; there is a left turn followed shortly by a right filter-road on to the A6. Continue for 1½ miles (2.4km) and turn left on to the A623, signed 'Chesterfield and Sheffield'. The landscape is quite different now; limestone country on a gently rolling plateau. After a mile (1.6km) the road bears sharp right then continues through high pastureland, cobwebbed by drystone walls, for 6 miles (9.7km) towards Tideswell. (A detour of a few hundred yards

to the right leads to this pretty village, dominated by its ornate parish church.)

Continue along the A623 for another three quarters of a mile (1.2km), past a pond on the left, then for another 1½ miles (2.4km) past the turn for Foolow. The road now bears right and dips down into wooded Middleton Dale.

After 1½ miles (2.4km) turn left for **Eyam**, for a short detour to visit the famous 'plague village'. Continue on the A623 for half a mile (0.8km) into Stoney Middleton, then for three quarters of a mile (1.2km) to traffic lights. Go straight on, through Calver after 2 miles (3.2km) and then back to Baslow.

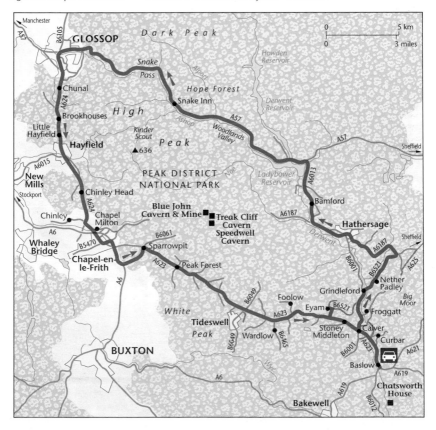

BRONZE-AGE FARMLAND
In the Bronze Age, the climate was mild and the ground was fertile; when archaeologists strip away the skim of soil from sites on the empty moors above the Derwent Valley they reveal a farmscape of fields and settlements. Clearly, there was nothing primitive about the people who lived here in those distant days – they made more of the land than we do.

CALVER AND CURBAR Derbyshire Map ref SK2574

The Derwent divides these shrinking communities; Calver on the west bank lies in the lee of the limestone hills, whilst Curbar sits below a gritstone edge, close to the moors. An 18th-century bridge links them, but this is now bypassed by a new crossing just downstream and most people never notice Curbar as they swing west to Calver Sough.

Calver has an industrial side to its character; shoes and sinks were among its products. The steel sink factory occupies what was once a cotton mill, built by Joseph Arkwright in 1805 and employing up to 200 people. The mill's moment of glory came in the 1970s when its satanic profile won it the role of Colditz Castle in the television series.

On the other side of the Derwent, Curbar is a quiet little place on the shoulder of pastureland before Curbar Edge. The older features of the village include a circular pinfold or stock-pound, a covered well and circular trough, and a lock-up with a conical roof. These structures survived because they were fashioned in stone and were built to last. In the 18th century nobody could foresee a time when sheep wouldn't stray, horses wouldn't be thirsty and men wouldn't get drunk.

The old Chesterfield turnpike heads east out of Curbar seeking the gap in the gritstone edge on the skyline. Stone slabs were easily won from the Edge and were used for more than millstones. On the tussocky pasture close to the village lies a group of gravestones marking the resting place of the Cundy family, who died of plague in 1632 (more than 30 years before the Eyam outbreak). Further up around the gap, several natural slabs of rock

Great slabs of stone adorn the horse trough in Curbar

bear biblical references, the work of a molecatcher-cum-preacher called Edwin Gregory, who worked on the Chatsworth Estate a century ago. Finally, as the road straightens and heads southeast over the Bar Brook, there are drystone walls, guideposts and a clapper bridge, dating back to the packhorse era before the road became a turnpike in 1759.

CHATSWORTH Derbyshire Map ref SK2670

Towards the end of the 17th century William Cavendish, 4th Earl of Devonshire and soon to be made the 1st Duke for his part in putting William of Orange on the throne, decided his house needed a radical new look. For a while he tinkered around with alterations, but finally knocked everything down and started again. Demolishing one great historic house to build another might seem an odd investment of a lifetime, but in those far-off days great families were judged by their homes and gardens; fashion and taste was everything.

The Chatsworth House that rose from the rubble of the Elizabethan mansion was of a classical, Palladian style, to the Duke's own design. It took about 30 years to complete and it set the seal on his new status – even some of the window frames were gilded on the outside. The irony is that he never saw it at its best. Great houses needed great gardens and grounds, and these took decades to establish. In the middle of the 18th century 'Capability' Brown and James Paine laid the foundations of what we see today by altering the course of the river and roads, building bridges and setting out wonderful woodland vistas.

Graceful landscaping and a picturesque bridge complete the classic view of this classic stately home

CHATSWORTH DEER

The park deer at Chatsworth are fallow deer, introduced into Britain by the Normans to grace their hunting forests. Fallow differ from the native red and roe deer in having a spotted coat and broad antlers. The parkland around Chatsworth sometimes gives the impression of an English version of the Serengeti, with cattle, sheep and deer in place of wildebeest and impala.

*Formal gardens surround
Chatsworth House*

BILBERRY TIME
Purple bird droppings on
moorland walls are a sign that
it is bilberry time. Bilberry
(called blaeberry in Scotland
and blueberry in America)
grows on the slopes and
along the road verges of
Beeley Moor. The bell-shaped
flowers give way to dark
purple berries in July; they are
inconspicuous and are often
overlooked, and the bushes
are soon stripped by grouse,
foxes and other wild animals.
But half an hour of gathering
should produce enough fruit
for a small pie. The taste is
unique and delicious.

The house is bursting with great works of art in the
most superb settings; the Painted Hall is a work of art in
itself, with huge, swirling scenes from the life of Julius
Caesar by Louis Laguerre on the ceiling and upper part of
the walls. Splendour follows splendour as you progress
through the house (a tour of about a third of a mile), but
one of the most engaging features that stays in the
memory of visitors long after they have departed is the
wonderfully realistic *trompe l'oeil* painting of a violin on
the inner door of the State Music Room.

None can deny the magnificence of the house itself,
but the secret of Chatsworth is its setting. From any
direction it looks majestic, and from the southwest,
approaching Edensor on a sunny evening, it can be
breathtaking. On the horizon to the east are the high
gritstone moors; in the middle distance are tiers of
woodland, melting into ribbons and stands of beech and
oak and rolling parkland; and in the foreground winds
the Derwent. The front of the house reflects the peach-
glow of evening sunlight to perfection; around it are
formal gardens and the great Emperor fountain. This is a
view the 1st Duke could only have dreamed about.

The Chatsworth Estate stretches far and wide and includes grouse moors, working farmland and estate villages. Of the villages Edensor catches the eye first. In fact it is a testament to the glorious megalomania of the 19th century: until the 1830s the village stood a little closer to the river but the 6th Duke had it moved further back, out of sight. The new houses were a hotchpotch of styles; Italian, Swiss, almost anything but vernacular English. Only one house of the original village remains, called Park Cottage, but known at one time as Naboth's Vineyard. The biblical reference relates to the owner in 1838 who is supposed to have refused to sell or be relocated. A mile (1.6km) to the northwest lies Pilsley, a more compact village than Edensor and with the benefit of both a public house (the Devonshire Arms) and the famous Chatsworth Farm Shop.

Just outside the grounds of the Chatsworth Estate to the south, but within its influence and historic ownership, lies Beeley (see Walk on page 78). Being a working village, tucked away and with elements of a much older settlement, it has a refreshingly stolid character. A tannery once stood beside the brook, and there was an estate-built school and a barn to house the coal wagons, supplying the Chatsworth glasshouses with fuel. Over the years most of the old buildings have been put to other uses, but not the public house (another Devonshire Arms!) which is still a good stopping place on the way up to the moors.

WILDLIFE OF THE MOORLAND

Of all the heather moorland in the Peak District the expanse above Beeley is probably the best for wildlife. This has been due in part to its isolation and lack of access, but paths are now open and it is possible to explore several of the finest routes without damaging the most sensitive ecological sites. It isn't even necessary to walk far to find moorland wildlife; the roadside walls are often the best places to look. Beautiful lichen-coloured moths like the grey chi and glaucous shears sit camouflaged on the stones, and the full-grown caterpillars of emperor and northern eggar moths like to sun themselves on the very tops of bilberry and heather clumps.

The Devonshires have thrown their home open not only to summer visitors, but during World War II to a girls' school, who took over many of the great rooms for classrooms and dormitories

Chatsworth and Beeley

This walk makes the most of the mansion's unrivalled setting, leading from the River Derwent to the village of Beeley, up the Beeley Brook to a wild sweep of heather moorland then back down through woodland and parkland and over riverside pastures.

Time: 3½ hours. Distance: 6½ miles (10.5km).
From November to March the path which runs from the Hunting Tower down beside the house is closed; the alternative route adds an extra half hour, and 1¼ miles (2km), to the walk.
Start: From Baslow drive south on the B6012 for about 3 miles (4.8km). Park at Calton Lees car park, just before Beeley Bridge.
(OS Grid ref: SK259685.)
OS Map: Outdoor Leisure 24
(The Peak District – White Peak area) 1:25,000.
See Key to Walks on page 121.

ROUTE DIRECTIONS

From the car park walk down the main road and trun right to cross Beeley Bridge, turn right through a kissing wicket on the right and follow the path across pastures towards **Beeley** village. Go through another kissing wicket, cross the road and walk into Beeley passing the church on the left. Turn right at the T-junction, walk downhill towards the Devonshire Arms. Turn left on the road beside Beeley Brook.

Cross a stone footbridge over the brook, go upstream, re-cross at another bridge in a few yards, and continue upstream on the road. As the road swings down and right to Moor Farm go straight ahead on a green track to a gate. Beyond the gate keep to the track on the outside of the wall enclosing woodland, ignoring two gates into the wood. When the track leads out into a field go through the gate ahead into the wood. The path descends, then climbs with a wall to the left. Cross a stream and follow the path which bears right through birch and conifers. Soon Beeley Brook is on the right again, heard if not seen. Ignore side paths.

At a large flat boulder keep uphill, close to the brook. Pass a broken bridge and in a few yards, at a tiny footbridge, turn sharp left away from the brook. Continue to the edge of the wood and out on to a track. Cross it to a stone stile, and along the track opposite bear left across the moor. Follow the broad track downhill through **The Warren** to a gate, cross a stone stile into a wood. Keep on this concessionary path, granted by the Trustees of the Chatsworth Settlement, and go straight on at a crossroads signposted 'Robin Hood'.

The track winds through woodland passing lakes until the **Hunting Tower** comes into view. There are two options from here. The private path (open April to October) cuts directly downhill past the house. To follow this, turn left along a grassy avenue to the Tower. Cross the road below the Tower, descend very steep steps and cross a track to a tarmac road. Turn right to pass Chatsworth House and go over the river bridge. Turn left across the riverside fields for almost a mile (1.6km) back to the car park.

In winter continue along the path above the Tower, turn right after 50 yards (45.7m) along a tarmac track signed 'Robin Hood'. After 300 yards (274m) bear left at the sign 'Concessionary Footpath – Baslow', go through the wood into Chatsworth Park. Bear diagonally right to an estate road, follow it to a junction and head across the park in the same direction towards a metal kissing gate in the far corner. Turn left, follow the riverside track to Chatsworth Bridge. Cross the bridge and turn left to cross the riverside fields for almost a mile (1.6km) back to the car park.

The Devonshire Arms at Beeley

POINTS OF INTEREST

Beeley
Many of the cottages in the village of Beeley wear the estate blue of Chatsworth and were built in the 19th century by estate architects.

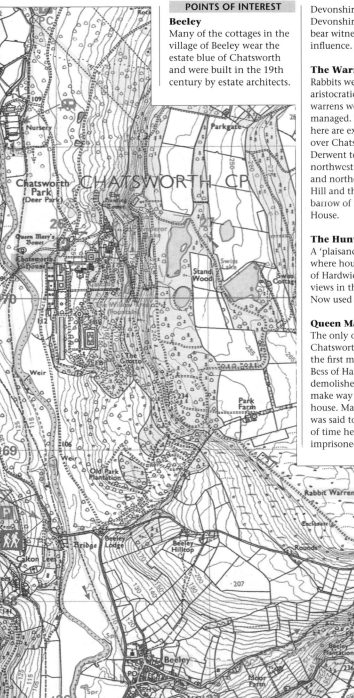

Devonshire Square and the Devonshire Arms pub also bear witness to the ducal influence.

The Warren
Rabbits were once an aristocratic dish and the warrens were carefully managed. The views from here are exceptional: west over Chatsworth and the Derwent to the White Peak, northwest to Curbar Edge and northeast to Bunker's Hill and the Bronze-Age barrow of Hob Hurst's House.

The Hunting Tower
A 'plaisance' or gazebo from where house guests of Bess of Hardwick enjoyed the views in the 16th century. Now used as a flag tower.

Queen Mary's Bower
The only other feature at Chatsworth remaining from the first mansion, built for Bess of Hardwick and demolished around 1700 to make way for the present house. Mary, Queen of Scots was said to have spent a lot of time here when imprisoned at Chatsworth.

Revolution House sporting a new crown of thatch, Old Whittington

MILLSTONE MARKERS

Most of the main roads into the Peak National Park carry boundary cairns, on which rest millstones of various shapes and sizes. These days the highways authority would have something to say about placing potentially dangerous stone blocks next to busy roads, but in the 1950s everyone was proud of the new Park and the planning authority was keen to give it a high profile.

CHESTERFIELD   Derbyshire Map ref SK3871

The spire of St Mary's and All Saints would have tapered to an elegant pencil-point if its timbers had been properly seasoned. Instead it stands crooked and twisted, a unique landmark, famous for the wrong reasons. Medieval Chesterfield was a prosperous town of guilds; it aspired to have a church worthy of its status and was full of fine buildings. Many of these still exist, hidden behind shop fronts and appearing whenever renovation tales place.

Chesterfield is an industrial town. Its heart still beats in time with the coalfields and it is worth visiting now for its old inns and good humour. It lies outside the Peak District, but serves its eastern flanks and is a popular gateway from the M1.

To the north of the town lies the village of Old Whittington, where a group of conspirators led by the Earl of Devonshire met in 1688 to hatch a plot to overthrow the Catholic King James II. The plot was successful; the country welcomed William of Orange and the course of history was changed. The meeting took place in a little thatched inn called the Cock and Pynot, now known as Revolution House and a modest tourist attraction, furnished in 17th-century style and with a video telling the story of the Revolution. Two miles (3.2km) away is Newbold Moor, where the tiny Norman Chapel was attacked in the same year by a Protestant mob. The chapel has recently been restored and has a simple weather-beaten charm. Near by is Tapton House, the home in later life of George Stephenson.

CRICH Derbyshire Map ref SK3454

Perched atop a limestone anticline, the monument on Crich Stand glows from a distance like a lighthouse set on alabaster cliffs above a shadowy sea. Three beacon-towers have stood on this same spot, but each time they were destroyed by lightning. The present structure dates from 1921 and is a memorial to the men of the Sherwood Foresters Regiment killed in the two world wars. The 63-foot (19m) tower is open to the public and affords breathtaking views across eight counties.

Below the Stand lies a working quarry, still eating away at the hill. In its early years George Stephenson built a narrow-gauge railway so that the limestone could be carried to kilns at Ambergate. Now, the worked-out shelf of the quarry is the home of the National Tramway Museum, where over 40 trams from all over the world are housed. Several are in working order and run every few minutes through a period street, then up on to open countryside. Along the street is the Georgian façade of Derby Assembly Rooms, relocated here in 1972 after the original building in Derby's Market Place had been damaged by fire. Other attractions here are many, and include an enormous exhibition hall and the high-tech sound and vision experience, Tracks in Time.

Crich village is a quiet little place; many of the houses date back to the 18th or early 19th century and were the homes of stockingers, working on knitting frames by the light of top-storey windows. The Jovial Dutchman dates from about the same time; the pub is named after the Dutch navvies who built Cromford Canal.

BIRDS OF PREY IN THE PEAK
Kestrels are never very far away from Crich Stand; they hunt the surrounding pastures for field voles and are easy to identify because of their habit of hovering. But other birds of prey nest in the Peak District, in the valley woods or on the moors. These include merlin, peregrine, hobby, hen harrier, sparrowhawk and goshawk – an impressive list considering the pesticide devastation of the 1950s.

Unassuming Crich is home to the delightful National Tramway Museum, offering excursions daily

The Cromford Canal was once a vital link in the network of industrial waterways

A CANAL NATURE RESERVE
Downstream of the Leawood viaduct the Derwent Valley is particularly beautiful; wild daffodils grow on the riverside pastures and the oakwoods ring with the sound of wood warblers, redstarts and pied flycatchers. Below Whatstand-well the overgrown canal is a local nature reserve and is a haven for old-fashioned wildlife; frogs and grass snakes, kingfishers and dragonflies.

By taking the train to Ambergate it is possible to walk along the towpath all the way to the next station at Whatstandwell, where there is an excellent pub.

CROMFORD Derbyshire Map ref SK2956

Road, rail, river and canal run side by side south from Cromford. At first sight it is hard to understand why transport was so important to the place – until 1771 it had been little more than a cluster of cottages around an old packhorse bridge. Then Richard Arkwright arrived and set to work to build a cotton mill. Power was plentiful, in the shape of Bonsall Brook and Cromford Moor Sough (the drainage waterway from nearby lead workings) and there was a ready supply of cheap labour because of the decline of the lead-mining industry. Within a few years Arkwright was rich and the village was a cradle of the Industrial Revolution; three mills were built and terraces of gritstone houses accommodated a workforce who laboured in factories rather than in their own homes, for long hours and to set shifts. For good and ill the Satanic Mills were the birthplace of the urban working class.

Cromford Canal was built in the early 1790s to link up with the Erewash Canal, which then ran southeast to Nottingham. Cromford Wharf marked its northern terminus, at the Arkwright Mill. A turnpike road was opened up in 1817, then in the 1830s the Cromford and High Peak Railway was constructed, which linked the Cromford Canal with the Peak Forest Canal at Whaley Bridge, thus linking the Trent with the Mersey. In its early years this 33-mile (53-km) wagonway employed horses on the level stretches and steam winding engines on the inclines. It was considered an extension of the canals and the stations were called wharfs, but by the middle of the 19th century the age of steam had arrived and the Midland Railway was extended north from Ambergate to meet the High Peak line.

Arkwright's Cromford Mill is now undergoing a major restoration programme by the Arkwright Society, who aim to create a lasting monument to his extraordinary genius. There are guided tours, and a visitor centre on the site interprets the mill's heyday. Cromford Canal is popular for family picnics, and there is a towpath walk to High Peak Junction, where there is another visitor centre. The Cromford and High Peak Railway closed in 1967 and is now a popular walkway, called the High Peak Trail. In post-industrial Britain the scars on the land have their own fascination.

Cromford is made prettier by its large pond, situated behind the market square, and the Greyhound Hotel (built by Arkwright in 1778). The pond was one of the impounding reservoirs to hold water from the Bonsall Brook, but its reedy margins are now the home of ducks and swans. On the other side of the A6, close to the wharf and within sight of Arkwright's elegant homes of Rock House and Willesley Castle, lies the old bridge and its ruined chapel, at the site of the 'crooked ford' that became Cromford. A lot of water has passed beneath its ancient arches.

THE BRIDGE CHAPEL AT CROMFORD

Cromford (pronounced 'Crumfud' by most locals) grew up around a crooked ford, and the old bridge still boasts a little chapel, where travellers gave thanks for a safe crossing. Most of the medieval village disappeared with the Industrial Revolution and the will of the powerful Arkwright family.

The pond and old water mill at Cromford

THE ANCIENT YEW

Churchtown, on a step above the Derwent, was a settlement in prehistoric and Roman times, and when the Saxons first held religious services here they probably gathered around an old yew tree. When they built a church they sited it next to the tree, and over the centuries each rebuilt church has stood in the shade of the same tree. Amazingly, this venerable yew survives to this day, a scruffy goliath with a 33-foot (10m) girth, one of the oldest trees in Britain. If only it could talk...

Darley Dale's church rewards a closer look

DARLEY DALE Derbyshire Map ref SK2663

Four settlements along the Derwent were bound together under the name of Darley Dale a century ago, but the ties were never strong enough to give the place a corporate identity. The A6 has now replaced the railway as the nub of the community, leaving Darley with an artery but no heart.

Darley (see Walk on page 86) was the home of Sir Joseph Whitworth, the man who invented the screw thread. Munitions (including a rifle that fired hexagonal bullets), machine tools, nuts and bolts soon made him rich, and he bestowed much of his wealth on the local community by building a Whitworth Hospital, a Whitworth Hotel, a Whitworth Park and a Whitworth Institute. Victorian benefactors liked to have their good deeds recognised, but in Whitworth's case his generosity won him few friends and he was not popular. He lived at Stancliffe Hall (not open), guarding his privacy behind high walls and hedges, and when he died in 1887 his dreams of a model village died too.

Beside the A6 lies Stancliffe Quarry, and stone from here was sent to London, where it was used to pave

Trafalgar Square and the Embankment. Below this, on the other side of the railway line and on a low mound above the river flats, is Churchtown. Here stands the parish church of St Helens, founded by the Normans but rebuilt in the 14th century, at the same time as the Old Hall which once stood a little way to the north. Most of what is visible on the outside is the result of Victorian restoration, but there are lots of interesting things to see inside; Saxon stones, painted wall designs, the tomb of Sir John de Darley (heart in hands), the private pew of the reclusive Sir Joseph Whitworth. The south transept has a superb stained-glass window by William Morris and Co, produced in the 1860s. The scenes are from the 'Song of Solomon', the chunky figures designed by Burne-Jones and the angels probably by Morris himself. Victorian stained glass doesn't come any better. (The church is locked when not in use, but a key-holder's telephone number is posted in the porch.)

Above Darley and Northwood lie open fields and woodland before the Derwent meets the Wye at Rowsley. These days the village of Rowsley is most notable as a gateway to the Peak National Park on the A6, but it used to be a railway village with marshalling yards and a dairy (to serve London, via the milk train). The railway closed in the late 1960s and the Station Hotel is now the Grouse and Claret. Near by is the Peacock Hotel, a 17th-century manor house, and the Caudwell Mill, a turbine-driven corn mill. The 19th-century mill has been adapted into a craft centre but it still makes bread, and visitors can stroll along the paths beside the mill race and along the Wye.

The yew in Darley churchyard is some 2,000 years old, and believed to be one of the oldest trees in Britain

WILD FLOWERS WITH WONDERFUL NAMES
Country names for wild flowers are often quaint and descriptive. Stonecrop and lords-and-ladies grow in the old walls and hedgerows on the slopes above the Derwent and rejoice in the old cottage names of 'Welcome-home-husband-though-never-so-drunk' and 'Kitty-come-down-the-lane-jump-up-and-kiss-me'.

Wensley Dale and Oker Hill

Not the Wensleydale of cheese fame, which is in North Yorkshire, but a little-known gem at the eastern edge of the White Peak plateau. Oker Hill is a grassy knoll offering splendid views; the ascent is short and only moderately steep.

Time: 2½ hours. Distance: 4 miles (6.4km).
Location: 5 miles (8km) northwest of Matlock.
Start: From Matlock drive northwest on the A6, turn left on to the B5057 at Darley Dale. Limited parking at Darley Bridge along the gated road to Oker. (OS Grid ref: SK271620.)
OS Map: Outdoor Leisure 24
(The Peak District – White Peak area) 1:25,000.
See Key to Walks on page 121.

ROUTE DIRECTIONS

From **Darley Bridge** follow the main road through the village towards Wensley, turn right into Oldfield Lane signed 'Stanton Lees and Enthovens'. Walk along the lane uphill. When the lane forks, take the smaller left fork and continue to a stile on the left, opposite a gate, to the rear of the Enthovens works. Cross the stile and go down to a footbridge in a little wooded valley. The path rises and merges with a broad track, follow this uphill; when it turns left continue ahead through a stile. Cross the field to another stile midway along the hedge opposite, go through a gate in the next field and into a lane leading into **Wensley.**

Cross the road making for a stile beyond the left side of Wensley Hall, bear right to a gate and turn left into a lane. Continue downhill, turn left and follow the path down the centre of **Wensley Dale**. When it levels out at the bottom, bear right in front of a small stone building into a

lane. Continue beside a wall on the left to a stile, cross this and follow a wall, now on the right. Continue across fields towards the left edge of the houses of Snitterton.

Before the village turn left,

away from a copse of trees, cross a small wooden bridge, walk beside a hedge on the right to a road. Turn left along it, bear right at a fork into Ashton Lane. After 50 yards (46m) turn left over a stile, follow an indistinct path uphill to the right-hand corner of the field through scrubby woodland to a lane. Turn right and after a few yards, when the lane peters out (well before the ruined building), climb the bracken-covered ridge on the left to a large sycamore on **Oker Hill**.

Continue along the ridge crest to the triangulation column at the far end. Descend the grassy slope to a five-bar gate, go through this and turn right down the road. Turn right into Flint Lane, and at the bottom where it forks, bear left. After about 50 yards (46m) continue along an unmetalled lane. Cross a stile on the left and follow the left edge of the field. Cross to the end of a hedge in the next

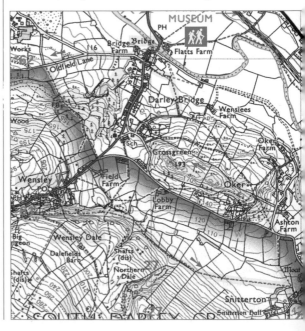

field, then turn left through a stile. Keep to the right edge of a sports field, then along a little lane leading from the right-hand corner. Walk through the car park of the Three Stags Heads Inn on to the main road. Turn right, back to Darley Bridge.

POINTS OF INTEREST

Darley Bridge
This two-arched stone bridge was built in the 15th century at the only suitable crossing place on the Derwent between Matlock and Rowsley. The river meanders through pasture-land, prone to flooding.

Wensley
A quiet village of stone cottages and pretty gardens. Where the path meets the road, look for a dovecote built into the gable end of a house. Before the advent of turnips to feed livestock over the winter, people kept pigeons for the pot.

Wensley Dale
A handsome sweep of dry valley grassland on the very edge of the limestone. The hawthorn bushes on the upper slopes are a sign that the rabbit population was at a low ebb when the saplings were young.

Oker Hill
Wordsworth wrote a poem inspired by the tale of two brothers who climbed Oker

Looking out from Oker Hill over Darley Dale

Hill and planted two trees on the crest before going their separate ways. Local legend has it that one of the trees flourished and the other died; certainly only one of the original trees survives, slightly bent against the wind.
The grass-covered mounds on the slopes of the hill are made by colonies of meadow ants. They spend most of their time below the surface, but often cluster around the southeast edges of the mounds in the early morning to enjoy the sun's warmth.

'TIN TOWN'

Car parks and cycle hire make it easy to explore the west side of the Derwent Valley, along the shores of all three reservoirs and through the forest. By Derwent Reservoir and just south of Birchinlee the road passes alongside the site of 'Tin Town', once a settlement of corrugated iron houses provided for the navvies who built the upper reservoirs. For a decade at the turn of the century it was a self-contained community a thousand strong, with its own school and railway station; all that remains are a few grass-decked foundations and terraces.

The massive Ladybower Reservoir provides water for cities in four counties

THE DERWENT DAMS Derbyshire

Engineers had their eye on Derwent Dale for decades before work began at Howden Reservoir in 1901. It was the perfect spot; a long deep groove through solid millstone grit, bleak rain-washed moors all around, and only a scattered farming community to relocate. After Howden came Derwent Reservoir, completed in 1916. Ladybower, the last and largest, was inaugurated in 1945; as well as flooding 2 miles (3.2km) of the Derwent valley this also spread up the Woodlands Valley, but not very far because of the risk of landslips. Ladybower (see Walk on page 96) now holds about 6,000 million gallons of water, the others slightly less; more than a third of the water goes to Leicester, another third to Sheffield, and the rest is shared between Derby and Nottingham.

Although the sheer scale of the engineering works is impressive, it is the creation of a Canadian-style landscape that draws visitors; big views over great sheets of water, curtains of mist and conifers decked in snow. Definitely not British, but a grand prospect. The forest looks dark and dreary, and there is no doubt that alien conifers are not a substitute for native oak when it comes to bio-diversity. Even so, there are a few surprises. Red squirrels keep a toe-hold here, and in good seed years the local chaffinches are joined by flocks of crossbills. Goshawks are widespread but furtive, except in the early spring when they soar high in display flight over the wooded cloughs.

The Derwent Dams are famous for their drowned villages; when there is a drought thousands of people flock to see a few uncovered stones. The only building to cheat the flood was the Derwent packhorse bridge, dismantled and rebuilt further up the valley to span the river at Slippery Stones.

Sketching by Burbage Brook, Grindleford

Sad heroic stories cling to the valley. One relates to two brothers buried in a snow avalanche whilst tending sheep on Whinstone Lee Tor; their dog ran home to Riding House Farm and a rescue was mounted which saved one of the brothers' lives. More poignant was the story of Joseph Tagg and his dog Tip. The old farmer had been missing for 15 weeks over the winter of 1953–4 when his body was found up on Howden Moors. Tip was still by his side, loyal to the end and only just alive. A stone memorial to the faithful collie stands near Derwent Dam wall.

GRINDLEFORD Derbyshire Map ref SK2477

The best way to arrive at Grindleford is by train, either from the west, through the 3½ mile (5.6km) Totley tunnel (the second longest in the country) or from the east, back-tracking down the line from Hathersage along one of the prettiest sylvan stretches of the Derwent. Before the advent of the Hope Valley line Grindleford was little more than a turnpike crossing (the toll house still stands, next to the bridge), and the nearby settlements of Upper and Nether Padley were small enough to be lost among the trees. But the villages blossomed with the opening of the railway station in 1898; most of the houses jostling the slopes and terraces were built by the resulting wave of Sheffield commuters, but not so many houses that the villages merged or lost their backdrop of woodland.

Grindleford Station is actually in Upper Padley. A few hundred yards towards the Derwent, over Burbage Brook and past the converted watermill, lie the ruins of Padley Hall. Very little remains of the 14th-century mansion except foundations. It was once the proud home of the Fitzherbert family, who were Roman Catholics and had the misfortune to be caught harbouring priests at a time

BIRDSONG IN THE GORGE

On still evenings in the woodland of Padley Gorge, listen for the drumming of woodpeckers and the strange roding call of the woodcock. Sounds carry a long way through the treetops, creating the hushed atmosphere of a cathedral.

OAK TREES

Sessile oak, with long leaf stalks and short acorn stalks, replaces pedunculate oak in the north and west of Britain and is the dominant tree of Padley Gorge. Pedunculate oak has always been more popular among foresters because it produces a more reliable crop of acorns. This is the main reason for its being the more common tree over most of the Peak District.

Padley Chapel, the site of an annual pilgrimage, was once the gatehouse to the old hall

when it was illegal to celebrate Mass. In fact the timing could not have been worse; the Spanish Armada had set sail and the whole country was on the lookout for spies. The two priests, Nicholas Garlick and Robert Ludlam (both local men who had been trained in France), were taken to Derby where they were hung, drawn and quartered. John Fitzherbert died in the Tower 30 years later. Padley Hall became the home of one of Queen Elizabeth's chief priest-catchers before being turned into a farm. The gatehouse, which had survived as a barn, was restored in 1933 and is now a chapel; a pilgrimage in memory of the martyrs takes place each July.

In the other direction, following the Burbage Brook upstream, runs a network of paths through Padley Gorge (see Walk on page 94). The boulder-strewn slopes of the gorge are covered in a thick layer of mosses and ferns, thriving in the damp shadows of the ancient oak wood. The trees are sessile oaks rather than pedunculate oaks; the obvious difference is that the sessile acorns are 'sessile' and don't have stalks. Acorns are an autumn bonanza for birds and animals; badgers and squirrels, jays and woodpigeons all make the most of the easy pickings. The spring bonanza is the crop of caterpillars, gathered from the opening leaves by migrant birds such as pied flycatchers and wood warblers.

Padley Gorge is part of the National Trust's Longshaw Estate. Longshaw Lodge, built as a shooting box for the Dukes of Rutland, stands beside the B6521 in attractive grounds. These are now the core of a country park, from where there is access to the moorland above Froggatt Edge. The views all along this most famous Edge are superb, westward over the White Peak and the Dark. To the east rises White Edge on Big Moor, running south to Swine Sty, a Bronze-Age settlement in a 'fossilised' landscape of prehistoric fields, picked out among beds of bracken and heather.

HATHERSAGE Derbyshire Map ref SK2381

Stanage Edge divides featureless moorland from the verdant Derwent. Prehistoric pathways, Roman roads and packhorse trails criss-cross the moors and converge below the confluence of the Derwent and the Noe. On the raised south-facing shoulder of the valley lies Hathersage ('Heather's Edge'), a village built on passing trade and farming. Millstones were a local speciality in the 18th century, hewn directly from quarry faces. Then came the Industrial Revolution and five mills were built, to make pins and needles. The mills had a short life, as did the men who ground the needle-points and had to breathe in the dust.

Whether there ever was a real Little John, or John Nailor, hardly matters; clearly, there should have been, and most visitors want to believe that it really is his grave they see in Hathersage's churchyard. There is no doubt that a suitable cap and bow once resided in the church, but they were of medieval rather than Saxon origin. The grave close to the south porch has been excavated several times without producing any bones, though there is a story that a huge thighbone was unearthed here in 1784. In fact the half-hidden stones at the head and foot of the grave were probably set there as the village perch: the standard measure used to mark out acres of land in the days of open-field or strip farming.

The most interesting buildings in Hathersage are along the main road and off School Lane. Past 15th-century Hathersage Hall and Farm, and up the narrow Church Bank, it is possible to walk around Bank Top, a knoll overlooking the alder-lined Hood Brook and valley. The church crouches on the grassy brow. To the south stands Bell House and The Bell Room, once an inn and barn beside the village green and stocks; to the west stands the Vicarage, and to the east is Camp Green, the ramparts of a 9th-century stockade. The north wind whistles through the tall lime trees in the churchyard, a reminder that Stanage and the high moors are only a couple of miles away.

MERRY MAN AND MAD WOMAN

Hathersage's lasting fame rests on two romances. The first involves Robin Hood, whose name can be found on anything from a nearby cave to a megalithic monument. Hood Brook divides the Dale (the old, interesting part of the village) from the new estate to the west; and in St Michael's churchyard is the grave of Little John. The other romance revolves around *Jane Eyre*. Charlotte Brontë stayed at the vicarage for three weeks in 1845 and spent much of her time listening to local gossip and visiting nearby houses. She wove truth and fiction together to create a parallel universe for her heroine. Tourists today like to chase the shadows by visiting North Lees, where Agnes Ashurst, the model for mad Mrs Rochester, once lived, or Moorseats, which was transmuted to Moor House. In the Brontë novel Hathersage is called Morton, a name borrowed from the landlord of the George Hotel.

The grave of Little John at Hathersage brings life to the tales of Robin Hood

The view across to Riber Castle and down over Matlock from the scenic Heights of Abraham, named for their likeness to the famous battle site at Quebec

A CANADIAN CONNECTION
The original Heights of Abraham are to be found above the precipitous Anse du Foulon, a mile (1.6km) north of Quebec in Canada. In 1759 a British force under General James Wolfe fought and beat the French by climbing the narrow path up to the rocky heights. Someone at a later date must have fancied a resemblance between the gorges of the Derwent and the St Lawrence.

MATLOCK   Derbyshire Map ref SK3059
Matlock is a tourist honeypot, but there is more to it than the fairy lights and family attractions. Old Matlock stands on the east bank of the Derwent, before it twists west, under the bridge. St Giles Church, the Rectory and Wheatsheaf House mark the original lead-mining settlement at the meeting of packhorse trails and turnpikes. Temple Mine is an old lead and fluorspar mine which is in the process of being restored to how it was in the 1920s and 30s, with a self-guided tour which illustrates its geology, mineralisation and mining techniques. Neighbouring Matlock Bath is the home of the Peak District Mining Museum.

Matlock Bath started as a petrifying well and tufa quarry, but in 1696 a bath was cut into the encrusted limestone and a spa was born. In the 18th and early 19th century the cream of society took the waters, staying in fashionable hotels on the sides of the gorge. Then in 1849 the railway arrived and the place was swamped by day trippers.

Matlock Bank, built on the gritstone/shale terraces facing you as you cross the bridge from the south, grew up around a hydropathic spa in the 1850s; the spa was the brainchild of a local mill owner called John Smedley and it made use of soft water, for bathing in, rather than the thermal spring water available down the road at Matlock Bath. In the early years of the 20th century there were 20 hydros on Matlock Bank and the steep streets had their own tram system.

Today, families come to the Matlocks to visit the popular Gulliver's Kingdom theme park which is divided into five different worlds each offering many rides and attractions, or to take a cable car up to the Heights of Abraham, with its showcaves, nature trail, water gardens and Owl Maze. Regardless of the other attractions, the cable car ride is worth taking for the magnificent views down the gorge.

ENTOMOLOGISTS DELIGHT
The northern brown argus butterfly is a speciality of the Peaks – this is as far south as it gets in Britain.

Houses crowd the gorge side at Matlock Bath

![walking symbol]

Padley Gorge and Froggatt Edge

This walk reveals the very best of the gritstone landscape, high moorland and a famous 'Edge' looking out west over the White Peak, some of the most beautiful oak woodland in the country and even some millstones along the way.

Time: 5 hours. Distance: 8½ miles (13.7km).
Location: 3 miles (4.8km) southeast of Hathersage.
Start: From Hathersage take the A6187 towards Sheffield.
Opposite the Fox House turn right signed 'Chesterfield (B6051)
and Dronfield'. Turn right into the Longshaw Estate. Park at the
National Trust car park. (OS Grid ref: SK267800.)
OS Maps: Outdoor Leisure 24 (The Peak District – White Peak)
1:25,000. Outdoor Leisure 1 (The Peak District – Dark Peak)
1:25,000 (Start point only shown on this map, not main walk.)
See Key to Walks on page 121.

ROUTE DIRECTIONS

From the car park take the path to **Longshaw Lodge Visitor Centre**. Pass in front of the Centre, take the left-hand path through open woodland for a mile (1.6km). Turn right on a clear path down open moorland towards a wooded valley below. Just before the trees, turn left and cross a stream. Walk by the wall bounding the wood.

At the top, where a small gate on the right leads into the wood, turn left through a

Padley Gorge, seen from Froggatt Edge

gate and continue towards a rock outcrop. Go through a wicket gate in the right-hand corner of the field and turn left along a path at the foot of the rocks (*not* sharp left with the wall). Curve round the outcrop and enter birch woodland. Fifty yards (46m) after a rock pinnacle, take a right fork downhill through the woods. Continue to the right of a parking area, and go up to the road.

Turn right for a few yards then left through a wicket gate on to a concessionary path along **Froggatt Edge**. At first the path is separated from the Edge by woodland, but there are opportunities to divert to viewpoints. Pass a massive jumble of rocks. Where the wall turns left, turn right on a path descending below the crags. Notice the millstones here. With a huge square pinnacle ahead, turn sharp left and descend steeply through woodland. Cross a

stile in a wall and continue to descend, curving to the right to a road.

Cross to a stile, cross a sparsely wooded field to a stile in the left-hand corner, turn right on to the road into Froggatt village. Pass the river bridge and go along Hollowgate. At the end of the village go ahead along Spooner Lane. After a squeeze stile bear right at the next corner of a wall to a stile opposite, continue along the left edge of the next field, then walk straight across to enter Froggatt Wood via another stile. When the path emerges from the wood keep along the left edge of a field, left through a wicket gate and cross to another on to the road by Grindleford Bridge.

Turn right and continue into Nether Padley. About 50 yards (46m) past the Maynard Arms Hotel bear left on a road signed 'Station'. Cross both the railway and Burbage Brook bridges, curve left past Padley Mill, turn right up a steep track then through a wicket gate into the woodlands of **Padley Gorge**. Continue to climb then take the left fork after a brief descent. After about ¾ mile (1.2km) through the gorge the path emerges from the woods and runs alongside the brook to a footbridge. Cross and bear right to a wicket gate, cross a road, go through another wicket a few yards down and enter Granby Wood. Keep to the left edge of the wood; skirt an ornamental pond and curve to the left, through a wicket, before returning to the Lodge and the car park.

POINTS OF INTEREST

Longshaw Lodge
A hunting lodge was first built here in the mid-18th century by the Duke of

Rutland; the turnpike road, now the A625, was diverted in the process. The Longshaw Estate was sold in 1927 and the house and grounds (now a country park) are administered by the National Trust.

Froggatt Edge

The face of Froggatt Edge, in a bower of autumn bracken and heather, is one of the most distinctive images of the Peak District. A stone circle and Bronze-Age burial grounds on the Edge suggest it has long been a place of ritual power. More recently it has attracted generations of climbers and walkers.

Padley Gorge

Ancient woodland, mainly composed of sessile oaks, flanks the sides of the Burbage Brook. In spring, just before the leaves hide everything in a dense green shade, this is a wonderful place for songbirds such as wood warblers and pied flycatchers.

Win Hill and Ladybower

A short strenuous walk up Parkin Clough is rewarded by panoramic views from the heather-clad cone of Win Hill. The rest is a gentle descent of the open ridge and a return along the forest edge above the shore of Ladybower Reservoir.

Time: about 4½ hours. Distance: 7 miles (11.3km).
Location: 3 miles (4.8km) northwest of Hathersage.
Start: From Hathersage take the A6187 west, turn right on to the A6013, pass the dam wall of Ladybower Reservoir and turn right into the Heatherdene car park.
(OS Grid ref: SK202858.)
OS Map: Outdoor Leisure 1 (The Peak District – Dark Peak area) 1:25,000.
See Key to Walks on page 121.

ROUTE DIRECTIONS

From the car park walk south through a gap in a wall and pass a picnic area. After 300 yards (274.3m) turn right and cross the road by the dam wall gates. Pass through the gap in the fence, take the stony path down through scrubby grassland. Bear left along the broad track and about 50 yards (46m) before the main gate bear right along a grassy path to the corner of the field and through a wicket gate. Turn right, cross Yorkshire Bridge, turn right again along a broad metalled track, with the river on the right.

After about 50 yards (46m) cross a stile beside a gate, then turn left up steps, cross a track and follow the steep path up Parkin Clough, ignoring any side paths. It is a tough, unremitting steep climb for the first 15 minutes or so. After crossing a forest road the gradient eases and a stile leads out of the plantation on to a track which continues to a clearing on the

skyline and up through heather. Over a stile, one more short steep section, then an easy stroll along the crest of **Win Hill** to the triangulation column and the summit.

Continue ahead over a heathery plateau, ignore a path to the left, and go straight on at a path crossing. Soon the path runs alongside a wall on the left. When the wall turns left carry on, following the path which curves right down the ridge to the forest edge. The path levels to cross a stile, continue between a wall and the forest boundary fence.

Descend to the **Guide Post**, (Hope Cross), on the left, cross a stile, turn right through a door (!) and descend through the forest to a glade and the ruins of farm buildings. Bear right past the first ruin, then left round other buildings and descend

steeply through the trees on a twisting path. More ruins are reached near the bottom, then a road and a bridge. Turn right along the road, at first following the River Ashop then continuing along the shore of Ladybower Reservoir to **Ladybower Dam**. Continue down the road to re-cross Yorkshire Bridge; then turn left at the wicket gate back into the field. Either follow the outward route back up to the toilet block or cross the track and follow a grassy path up between fields to the road, and a pub.

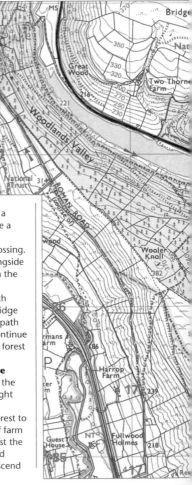

POINTS OF INTEREST

Win Hill

For such a modest height the views from heather-clad Win Hill are astonishingly good, particularly over the Hope Valley. Lose Hill, due west across the valley of the River Noe, is a few feet higher than Win Hill.

Guide Post

Also called the Hope Cross, this stone marker was erected in the year 1737 to guide travellers from the northwest into the Hope Valley. The path is on the line of an old Roman road, linking the forts at Hope and Glossop.

Ladybower Dam

The lower Woodlands Valley and Derwent Dale were

Descending through the forest at Win Hill

flooded in 1943 to create Ladybower Reservoir. The 140-feet (42.7m) high wall impounds over 6,000 million gallons of soft water from the Bleaklow/Kinder watershed, serving the very thirsty cities of Sheffield, Nottingham, Derby and Leicester.

The Derwent Valley and the Eastern Moors

✔ **Checklist**

Leisure Information

Places of Interest

Shopping

The Performing Arts

Sports, Activities and the Outdoors

Annual Events and Customs

Leisure Information

TOURIST INFORMATION CENTRES

Chesterfield
Low Pavement. Tel: 01246 345777/8.
Matlock Bath
The Pavilion. Tel: 01629 55082.

NATIONAL PARK INFORMATION

Peak District National Park
Head Office, Aldern House, Baslow Road, Bakewell.
Tel: 01629 816200.
www.peakdistrict.org.uk

OTHER INFORMATION

Derbyshire Wildlife Trust
Elvaston Castle, Derby.
Tel: 01332 756610.
English Heritage
Canada House, 3 Chepstow Street, Manchester. Tel: 0161 242 1400.
www. english-heritage.org.uk
English Nature
Manor Barn, Over Haddon, Bakewell. Tel: 01629 815095.
National Trust
East Midlands Regional Office, Clumber Park Stableyard, Worksop, Notts. Tel: 01909 486411.
High Peak and Longshaw Estate Office. Tel: 01433 670368.

www.nationaltrust.org.uk
Public Transport
The 'Derbyshire Wayfarer' allows one day's unlimited travel on local buses and trains in the county. Details from Derbyshire County Council, Public Transport Dept. Tel: 01629 580000.
Derbyshire Busline Tel: 01298 23098.
GMPTE Tel: 0161 288 7811.
South Yorkshire Travelline Tel: 01709 515151.
Rail information Tel: 0345 484950.
www.derbysbus.net
Severn Trent Water
2297 Coventry Rd, Birmingham. Tel: 0121 722 4000.
Staffordshire Wildlife Trust
Coutts House, Sandon, Stafford. Tel: 01889 508534.
Weather Call
Tel: 0906 850 0417.

ORDNANCE SURVEY MAPS

Landranger 1:50,000 Sheets 111, 119, 120.
Outdoor Leisure 1:25,000 Sheets 1, 24.

Places of Interest

There will be an admission charge at the following places of interest unless otherwise stated.

Caudwell's Mill and Craft Centre
Rowsley. Tel: 01629 734374. Open all year, daily. Free.
Chatsworth House
Tel: 01246 582204. Open Mar–Oct, daily.
Chesterfield Museum and Art Gallery
St Mary's Gate. Tel: 01245 345727. Open all year, most days. Free.
Cromford Mill
Tel: 01629 824297. Guided tours; visitor centre. Open all year daily except 25 Dec. Free.
Heights of Abraham
Matlock Bath. Tel: 01629 582365. Open Etr–Oct, daily.
Lea Gardens
3 miles (4.8km) southeast of Matlock, off A6. Tel: 01629 534380. Open late Mar to mid-Jul, daily.
National Tramway Museum
Matlock Road, Crich. Tel: 01773 852565. Open Apr–Oct, most days.
Nine Ladies Stone Circle
Stanton Moor. Open all year, any reasonable time. Free.
Peacock Information and Heritage Centre
Low Pavement, Chesterfield. Tel: 01246 345777. Open all year, most days. Free.

Peak District Mining Museum
The Pavilion, Matlock Bath.
Tel: 01629 583834. Open all year, daily.

Peak Rail
Matlock Station, Matlock.
Tel: 01629 580381. Trains run from Rowsley South to Matlock Riverside all year.

Revolution House
High Street, Old Whittington.
Tel: 01246 453554/345727.
Open mid Apr–Oct, daily. Free.

Temple Mine
Temple Road, Matlock Bath. Tel: 01629 583834. Open Oct–Mar, daily.

Whistlestop Countryside Centre
Old Railway Station, Matlock Bath. Tel: 01629 580958. Open Apr–Oct daily; weekends in winter. Free.

Working Carriage Museum
Red House Stables, Old Road, Darley Dale. Tel: 01629 733583. Open all year.

SPECIAL INTEREST FOR CHILDREN

The following places may be of interest to visitors with children. Unless otherwise stated, there will be an admission charge.

Chatsworth Farm and Adventure Playground
Tel: 01246 582204. Open late Mar–Sep; adventure playground also open weekends in Oct.

Gulliver's Kingdom
Temple Walk, Matlock Bath.
Tel: 01629 580540. Open Apr to mid-Oct most days; mid-Oct to Dec phone for opening times.

Matlock Bath Aquarium and Hologram Gallery
110 North Parade, Matlock Bath.
Tel: 01629 583624. Open Etr–Oct daily, winter wknds only.

Shopping

Chesterfield
General market, Mon, Fri and Sat; Flea market, Thu.

Matlock
General market, Tue and Fri.

LOCAL SPECIALITIES

Craft Centres
Derbyshire Craft Centre, Calver

Bridge. Tel: 01433 631231.
Cauldwell's Mill and Craft Centre, Rowsley. Tel: 01629 734374.

Cutlery
David Mellor Cutlery Factory & Country Shop, The Round Building, Hathersage. Tel: 01433 650220.

Flour
Cauldwell's Mill Trust, Rowsley, Matlock. Tel: 01629 734374.

Pottery
Crich Pottery, Market Place, Crich. Tel: 01773 853171.

The Performing Arts

Pomegranate Theatre, Corporation Street, Chesterfield. Tel: 01246 345222.
The Winding Wheel, Holywell Street, Chesterfield.
Tel: 01246 345333.

Sports, Activities and the Outdoors

ANGLING

Contact Severn Trent Water, 2297 Coventry Road, Birmingham. Tel: 0121 722 4968.

CRICKET

Derbyshire County Cricket Ground, Queens Park, Chesterfield. Tel: 01332 383211.

CYCLE HIRE

Bakewell
Peak Cycle Hire, National Park Office. Tel: 01629 815211.

Bamford
Derwent Cycle Hire, Fairholmes Car Park.
Tel: 01433 651261.

GOLF COURSES

Bamford
Sickleholme Golf Club, Saltergate Lane. Tel: 01433 651306.

Chesterfield
Chesterfield Golf Club, Walton. Tel: 01246 279256.

Matlock
Matlock Golf Club, Chesterfield Road. Tel: 01629 582191.

Stanedge
Stanedge Golf Club, Walton Hay Farm. Tel: 01246 566156.

GUIDED WALKS

National Park Walks with a Ranger
Contact Peak District National Park 24-hour information line
Tel: 01629 816327.

HORSE-RIDING

Chesterfield
Alton Riding School. Tel: 01246 590267.

Darley Dale
Red House Stables, Old Road.
Tel: 01629 733583.

LONG-DISTANCE FOOTPATHS AND TRAILS

The Limestone Way
Runs for 26 miles (41.8km) from Matlock to Castleton.

Annual Events and Customs

Bamford
Sheepdog Trials and Country Show, late May. Well-dressing and Carnival, mid-July.

Baslow
Well-dressing and Carnival, early July.

Chatsworth
Open-air concert with fireworks, early July. Horticultural Show, late August. Country Fair, early September.

Chesterfield
Festive Markets: Easter, Spring Bank Hol, late July, late August. Well-dressing early to mid-Sep.

Crich
Festival of Transport, late August.

Cromford
Steam Rally, held at Highacres, Farm Brackenfield, early August.

Grindleford
Carnival, mid-June. Horticultural Show, late August.

Hathersage
Horticultural Show, early September.

Matlock
Carnival, early to mid-August.

Matlock Bath
Illuminations, late August–October.

Rowsley
Well-dressing, late June.

Stoney Middleton
Well-dressing, with demonstrations, late July.

The Dark Peak

For six days out of every seven, cloud banks menace the desolate summits of Bleaklow, Black Hill and Kinder. Snow is almost as likely in June as in January; rain is inevitable. This is high country with a bed of millstone grit beneath the peat; on the surface is a skim of bog moss or cotton grass, the home of curlews and golden plovers. The Pennine Way tracks north along the backbone of England; only two or three roads chance their way across the wilderness. All of this adds to the attraction, and every now and then there is a sunny day and it is possible to stand on a bank of cloudberry and see for ever.

OAK APPLE DAY

Oak Apple Day, 29 May, is celebrated in Castleton by a glorious pub crawl, involving a procession led by the 'King' and 'Queen', both in Restoration costume and on horseback; the King is completely covered in a great cone of flowers. A silver band plays the traditional tune 'Pudding in a Lantern', girls dance and everyone welcomes the summer. This is Garland day; obscure, colourful and intoxicating. The words of a song capture the spirit of the event:
Thou doesno' know, and I dono' know
What they han i' Brada;
An owd cow's head, and a piece o' bread,
And a pudding baked in a lantern

Castleton is a good centre for exploring the Peak District caverns

CASTLETON Derbyshire Map ref SK1582

Castles and caves cast a potent spell; Castleton sometimes suffers from a surfeit of tourists, but there is so much of interest along the upper reach of the Hope Valley that it is impossible not to be drawn into the busy little village, at least as a base from which to wander.

The curtain of high hills at the head of the valley rises to 1,695 feet (517m) at Mam Tor, less than 2 miles (3.2km) to the northwest of the village. Bands of shale and gritstone give the breast-shaped dome of this 'mother-mountain' a terraced appearance; more importantly, the shale is unstable and the whole hillside is gradually slumping down into the valley, taking the old main road with it. In recent years the fate of the road has drawn as many sightseers as more conventional tourist attractions.

The tumbled stonework of an Iron-Age hill-fort rings the top of Mam Tor; hill-forts were a sign of prestige and status among hostile tribes in those faraway times, and this site must have been the power-base of an important chieftain. When the Romans arrived the local community had to learn a new way of life; from 'Celtic cowboys' of the open hills they became hewers and delvers in the dusty darkness of the lead mines.

Mining, for galena or lead ore, was a major industry in the Castleton area for the best part of 2,000 years, and it has left its scars. Grassy mounds and tree-lined ditches hide old spoil-heaps and rakes or veins. Many of the spoil-heaps were reworked for other minerals, such as fluorspar and blende, and natural limestone caves were enlarged or extended. Although the Derbyshire mines yield no silver, the area west of Castleton, up the winding road to Winnats Pass, is famous for its Blue John, a deep purple form of fluorspar.

The Treak Cliff, Speedwell and Peak Cavern 'show caves' are open to the public. Of these, Treak Cliff is an old lead mine, rich in veins of the mineral known as Blue John and is still worked, whilst the Speedwell Mine is special because the main workings (and the 'Bottomless Pit') can only be approached by boat, along an underground 'canal' or flooded tunnel. Peak Cavern lies close to Castleton, set into Castle Hill on the south side of the valley and with an enormous natural entrance – 100 feet (30.5m) across and 50 feet (15.2m) high. All the caves are exciting to explore, even in the company of a guided party.

The mighty bulk of Mam Tor towers to the northwest of Castleton

BLUE JOHN
Fluorite is a common mineral and its ore, fluorspar, has been mined in northern England for centuries. The pretty blue and yellow banded variety of the mineral, known as Blue John, has only ever been found in the Castleton caves. Some of the most beautiful decorative work was produced in the bowls and fireplace panels made in the 18th century, for Kedleston and Chatsworth. These days the veins are narrow, but it is still possible to buy small items of Blue John jewellery at the Castleon Gift Shop.

CASTLETON'S DRY VALLEY
Cave Dale, the deep gully protecting the east flank of Peveril Castle, is a classic example of a dry valley. It began life as a subterranean watercourse but the water gradually dissolved the limestone until there was a cavern. Eventually the roof fell in and what had been a cave became a valley.

A winding path leads through narrow Cave Dale, one of Peveril's natural defences

Castleton owes its name and very existence to Peveril Castle, perched on Castle Hill. It was built by William de Peverel, a favourite of William the Conqueror, in 1076. All mineral rights belonged to the king, who therefore had good reason to set a friend up with an overview of the lucrative lead-mining area. The castle also happened to be in the heart of the Peak Forest, prime hunting country; Normans liked to mix profit with pleasure. Meanwhile the Saxons hewed and delved below...

Peveril Castle is managed by English Heritage and is open to the public. The footpath up to it is steep and sometimes slippery because of frost, rain and sheep droppings, but the views from the curtain wall are exceptionally good. Cave Dale, a sheer-sided limestone gorge, forms a natural defence to the south and east; to the west is the wooded cleft of Peak Cavern and to the north is Hope Valley and the gritstone hills.

EDALE Derbyshire Map ref SK1285

Edale is the name given to the upper reaches of the River Noe as it threads its way through a broad valley of pastures and meadows. Five ancient farming communities, the Booths, are scattered along the north slope of the valley, tucked in beneath the desolation of the Kinder plateau but above the wilderness of the river. 'Booths' were barns or cowsheds, refuges for stock and farming families in troubled times; they have grown into hamlets and villages linked by green meadows and twisting lanes and an atmosphere of rural calm.

Grindsbrook Booth lies at the heart of the dale and can be anything but calm on sunny Sundays. Edale is the threshold of the high hills, the access point to Kinder. It marks the start of the Pennine Way, the first and most famous long-distance footpath in Britain, and is a magnet for walkers. Sitting outside the old Nag's Head Inn and watching a tide of seriously keen walkers disappearing up the track can be a little daunting; in fact most visitors to Kinder are only there for the day and only go a few miles. Of those intending to walk the whole 256 miles (412km) of the Pennine Way, most give up after the first day. The really testing ground is the high Kinder and Bleaklow plateau, a wilderness of sodden peat. But there is good walking on a firm track before that, from opposite the Nag's Head in the shade of a tall walnut tree, along a footpath signed Hayfield and westwards along the old packhorse trail.

This route, recently established as the official start of the Pennine Way, takes you through Upper Booth and up Jacob's Ladder, a set of zigzag steps cut into the hillside by an 18th-century 'jagger', or herder, who lived at Youngit Farm. Edale Cross marks the meeting of the three wards of the Royal Forest of the Peak, and then it is only a few hundred yards north to Kinder Low and Kinder Downfall, the famous waterfall that sometimes gets blown uphill in the teeth of the western gales. A stiff walk, but the views to the west are very special.

'WHETHER THE WEATHER BE WET'
Edale is not a place to linger in the rain; 60 inches (152cm) a year fall on Kinder, and the Booths get their share. Nor is there very much cover. On crisp winter mornings it can be cold in the valley, as frost rolls down from the summits, but this is certainly the time to appreciate the elemental landscape and the far horizons.

The picturesque Nag's Head is the place for a spot of 'Dutch Courage' before tackling the rigours of the Pennine Way

ROMAN GLOSSOP

Glossop's Roman fort, on the outskirts of the town and buried from sight, had its heyday during the advance of Agricola around AD 78. The local Brigantian tribes were no match for the garrison of Frisian auxiliaries and the badlands of the border were soon pushed well to the north; although the original wooden fort was replaced in stone around AD 140, it was soon deserted and most of the stone was pilfered by the local Brits for walls and barns.

Slender pillars support the tall arches of Glossop's Market Hall

GLOSSOP Derbyshire Map ref SK0393

Textiles breathed life into Glossop; there was water power and coal a-plenty and a willing workforce out of Stockport and Manchester. At the turn of the 19th century there were more than 56 mills in the eight townships of Glossopdale; most were cotton mills, but there were also paper mills, ropewalks and woollen mills. Not many thrived; those that did changed with the times and took to power looms, which were steam-driven and needed more water and more coal.

The settlement expanded in the early 19th century under the patronage of the Duke of Norfolk and at one time it was called Howard Town (Howard is the family name of the Duke), to distinguish it from Old Glossop, the village uphill to the east. The name Glossop came from Glott Hop, 'hop' being a valley and 'glott' a much earlier lord of the manor. But it was the Howards who left the greatest mark on the new community and who were responsible for most of the important buildings, such as the Market Hall and the Railway Station. The heart of Glossop is Norfolk Square, which still has a prim elegance about it and is surrounded by interesting shops, including a small heritage centre.

Glossop suffered disastrously when the cotton industry collapsed in the 1920s, and it took decades to recover. Overspill housing from the 1960s has affected the character of the town too, but there are some fascinating nooks and crannies, hidden away in the fabric of the place. Just beyond the housing estate of Gamesley lies the remains of the Agricolan Roman fort of Melandra Castle, whilst to the north of the town, near Howard Park, is Mouselow or Castle Hill, with important Bronze-Age and Iron-Age associations and the site of a motte and bailey built by William de Peverel. Glossop's roads to the east lead to Longdendale and the Snake Pass, whilst only a few miles to the west is the M67 and Manchester.

Glossop sprawls across the valley floor

FAMINE IN GLOSSOP
World events often have unexpected consequences, usually for the worse. The American Civil War increased the cost of raw cotton imports to Britain so much in the early 1860s that all the mills in Glossop closed and the townspeople suffered a disastrous famine.

Tintwistle and Longdendale

Longdendale is an oasis of green fields, woodland and blue water, chiselled out of a wilderness of moorland and blanket bog. Bleaklow, 2,060 feet (628m), and Black Hill, 1,909 feet (582m), gather their freezing mists to north and south, but the east–west dale is as sheltered a spot as you will find in the northern Peak. This walk makes a circuit of the lowest of the valley's reservoirs, climbing on to the shoulder of the moorland.

Time: 3 hours. Distance: 4½ miles (7.2km).
Location: 4 miles (6.4km) north of Glossop.
Start: From Glossop take the A57 northwest, then right along the A628 through Hollingworth to Tintwistle. Turn right opposite Church Inn, down New Road. Park on the roadside.
(OS Grid ref SK019972.)
OS Map: Outdoor Leisure 1
(The Peak District – Dark Peak area) l:25,000.
See Key to Walks on page 121.

ROUTE DIRECTIONS

From New Road in **Tintwistle** walk back to the main road (A628) and cross to the Church Inn. Turn right then bear left up the old village street to the village green. Bear left along the top of the green past the war memorial and take the left fork at the end of the village. In 50 yards (46m) take a path to the left, signposted 'Footpath to Open Country', which winds up into old quarry workings. Turn sharp right to another 'Open Country' signpost, and left uphill along the edge of the quarry to a ladder stile, beyond which is the boundary of open country or moorland. Keep on a well-defined path on the right-hand edge of the heather moor, winding through jumbles of rock debris. The path then bears right to contour just above the

walls enclosing the pastures below **Tintwistle Low Moor**. There are good views from here, over the reservoirs to Bleaklow and the Dark Peak.

At the corner of a wall follow the path downhill into a little valley until it merges with a broad track coming up from the right. Keep along this path, signed 'Bridleway', as it runs beside a wall on the right until it meets a broad stoney road. Follow this downhill to the A628. Cross carefully, obliquely to the left, and go down the road that leads over the dam between the Rhodeswood and Valehouse reservoirs. Turn right after the dam along the broad track past Deepclough Farm until you reach a gate on the left which leads up on to the **Longdendale Trail**.

Turn right along the Longdendale Trail and just

after drawing level with the beginning of **Bottoms Reservoir**, below on the right, bear left then turn right to pass under the trail. Go down to the bottom right-hand corner of the field and turn left along the wall by the shore of the reservoir. Go through a wicket gate to follow the shoreline to the dam.

From the top of the dam, go forward down to a road, turn right, then cross Tintwistle Bridge and continue up New Road to return to Tintwistle.

POINTS OF INTEREST

Tintwistle Village
The Top End of Tintwistle, standing high above the reservoirs and road, dates back at least 1,000 years, but most of the converted farm buildings and weavers' cottages along the little side-road, past the war memorial and village green, date from the 18th century. Families weaved on hand looms in their homes, the community expanded and the mills opened. Now most of the residents commute to Manchester. 'Tinsel', is the local pronunciation.

Tintwistle Low Moor
The view from the edge of Low Moor tells a story of endeavour in the face of adversity; Bleaklow, a soaking windswept desert, draped in clouds for most of the year, rises above the cattle pastures on the far side of the valley. To the east lies the string of reservoirs, gaining height as they recede.

Longdendale Trail
The long-distance footpath was once the busy Great Central Railway built to link Manchester to Sheffield. The famous Woodhead Tunnel, completed in 1847, was part of the scheme.

Bottoms Reservoir
The string of reservoirs along the bed of Longdendale was built by the Manchester Corporation in the middle of the 19th century. The three upper reservoirs, Woodhead, Torside and Rhodeswood, stored spring water to slake the thirst of the growing city. The two smaller reservoirs of Valehouse and

Longdendale contains a string of small reservoirs

Bottoms were intended for storm water, to regulate the flow to mills on the Etherow.

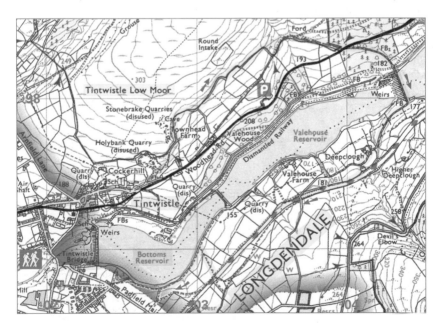

THE RIGHT TO ROAM

The Mass Trespass which took place on 24 April 1932 was a peaceful protest, but politically explosive, to gain access to the hills. About 500 walkers took part, climbing the public footpath out of Hayfield to William Clough. A brief scuffle took place when the protesters left the path and were met by a group of gamekeepers on Sandy Heys, but there was no real confrontation and nobody actually bothered to trespass to the top of Kinder. Even so, six protesters were arrested and thrown into the old Hayfield lock-up on Market Street. They duly appeared at Derby Assizes and were sentenced to up to six months in gaol, which resulted in a publicity bonanza for the ramblers and ensured a place in history for Hayfield and the 'right to roam'.

A charming terrace of cottages backs on to the beck at Hayfield

HAYFIELD Derbyshire Map ref SK0386

The pretty name and rural setting disguise Hayfield's industrial past; the village once hummed and rattled to the sound of cotton and paper mills, calico printing and dye works. It has also resounded to marching feet and cries of protest – in 1830 a mob of 1,000 mill workers gathered to demand a living wage and were dispersed by hussars. Eleven men appeared at Derby Assizes as a result but the cotton industry was in terminal decline and all the anger was in vain. A century later Hayfield was the starting point for the famous 'mass trespass' of ramblers on to Kinder Scout.

Despite the occasional flurries of excitement Hayfield is a peaceful little village, catering for tourists of all kinds. It is full of little cafés and restaurants with quaint and inventive names. One of the most revealing places to while away a few minutes is by the bridge, next to the courtyard of the Royal Hotel, which looks out over the River Sett, from the war memorial to the jumble of stone-built cottages and sloping roofs at the back of Church Street. Near by is St Matthew's Church, built on the foundations of an older church which was washed away in a flood.

Serious walkers head east out of the village, up and over the green foothills to the russet expanse of the Kinder plateau. Families and easy-going ramblers head west along the Sett Valley Trail towards New Mills. The car park at the start of this 3-mile (4.8-km) trail, separated from the main village by the A624, was once the railway station, and the trail itself follows the course of the single-track line. In its heyday thousands of day visitors arrived here from Manchester via the New Mills branch line; Hayfield marked the end of the mill towns and the start of the countryside.

HOLMFIRTH West Yorkshire Map ref SE1408

Before the long-running BBC television series *Last of the Summer Wine* became a national institution, the most famous comic characters to come out of Holmfirth were on the postcards published by Bamfords. Saucy seaside cartoons became a serious business for the family firm just after the Great War; they had already pioneered lantern slides and the motion picture industry but were outflanked in the end by Hollywood.

The town of Holmfirth is a gem, built at the confluence of the Holme and the Ribble, where the Norman Earl Warren built a corn mill. For several centuries the lower valley was left to the wild wood and the hilltop towns of Cartworth, Upperthong and Wooldale prospered, combining farming with weaving. There are some fine stone farmhouses and cottages on the upper slopes of the valley, often absorbed into the outskirts of the newer town, to tell the tale of prosperity (see Walk on page 112). With the expansion of the cotton mills in the mid-19th century tiers of three-storey terraced cottages sprang up lower and lower into the valley and eventually cotton mills crowded the riverside. The fast-flowing river itself was harnessed but never tamed; it still floods when the Pennine snows melt too quickly.

Holmfirth has to be explored at a gentle pace, because most of the streets are steep. From Victoria Bridge in the middle of the town it is possible to wander up Penny Lane, round the back of the church where the surrounding hills peep out between chimney-pots and sooty walls, and down cobbled lanes worn smooth by a million clogs. Somewhere along the way you are almost certain to arrive at Sid's Café, or The Wrinkled Stocking Café, next door to Nora Batty's on the riverside.

THE PENNINE WAY

When it is spring in the valley and there are daffodils all over Holmfirth it is sobering to look to the west and see the clouds still gathered over Wessenden and Saddleworth Moors, and the snow lying on the summit of Black Hill. It looks a frightening prospect, but thousands of walkers tackle it each year as part of the Pennine Way National Trail. The Pennine Way has existed for over 30 years, and in that time places like Featherbed Moss and Wessenden Head have gained a notoriety, quite deserved, for their evil bogs. These days most of the worst bits are stone-flagged, using old mill-floor sets to create causey paths like the old packhorse trails. Even so, the Pennine Way is a challenge, and the pubs and guesthouses of Holmfirth are a welcome diversion.

Despite recent television fame, Holmfirth retains its Yorkshire dignity

PEAK'S HOLE

Hope lies at the confluence of the Noe and Peakshole Water, which rises out of the bowels of the earth at Peak Cavern. In the earthy 18th century, the Peak Cavern was called Peak's Hole, or the Devil's Arse!

The squat spire of Hope church takes on rocket-like proportions from below

HOPE Derbyshire Map ref SK1783

The Hope Valley is the main access route from the Derwent Valley to Castleton, Edale and the Dark Peak, so the road is often busy. The little village of Hope lies at the confluence of the Noe and the Peakshole Water, which emerges from the bowels of the earth 2 miles (3.2km) away at Castleton. Hope railway station lies half a mile (0.8km) out of the village, across the Noe to the east, and is a perfect starting point for a walk up Win Hill, one of the best viewpoints in the whole Peak. Lose Hill, the dark twin of Win Hill and another fine viewpoint, lies due west on the opposite side of the Noe.

Hope Church is in the heart of the village and is a typically squat-spired affair, dating back to the 14th century. Inside are two stone coffin lids bearing hunting horns, the motif of royal forest huntsmen. Outside, next to the porch, is the shaft of a Saxon cross with vague weathered carvings on its face. Stone scroll-work on preaching crosses represents the height of Dark-Age culture and the Peak District has some fine examples.

South of Hope stands the Blue Circle cement works, undeniably a blot on the skyline and difficult to reconcile with a National Park except as a source of local employment (but perhaps tourists of the future will come specially to see it, just as today's visitors explore old lead workings and derelict mills). Other landscape features are dwarfed in the presence of this monolith, but it marks the dividing line between the gritstone and limestone; the fields to the south are bright green and enclosed in a mesh of dove-grey drystone walls.

The village of Bradwell lies only a couple of miles from Hope but it is completely different in character, full of steep twisty lanes and lead-miners' cottages. A ridge called the Grey Ditch climbs the slope to Rebellion Knoll and may be a trace of the boundary between the Dark-Age kingdoms of Mercia and Northumbria. Near by, accessible by a riverside path from Hope, lies the site of a Roman fort. There is little to see on the ground, the stonework having been plundered long ago to build local farmhouses and Hope church.

PEAK PASTURES

Most of the grass fields on the valley floor are cut as a fodder crop, to keep as winter feed for dairy cattle and sheep. Hay used to be the usual crop, cut in June or early July and stacked or baled dry. Silage is now much more widespread, the crop cut earlier and 'pickled' in big bags. Wild flowers can't survive in heavily fertilised silage fields, which accounts for the green monotony of some farmscapes. Special subsidies are now helping to reverse the trend, at least in National Parks.

Rails, roads and rivers all pass through the Hope Valley

Holmfirth

A walk through Holmfirth, its stonework blackened by
forgotten industries, tells one story; a climb up the
cobbled lanes, beside drystone walls, with pasture
after pasture rising out of the Holme Valley to the
towering moors, tells another. Holmfirth is an
engaging place and this walk sets
the town in its context.

Time: 3½ hours. Distance: 5 miles (8km).
Location: Holmfirth; 5 miles (8km) south of Huddersfield.
Start: Park in the car park off the A6024 (Huddersfield Road)
close to the town centre.
(OS Grid ref: SE143084.)
OS Map: Outdoor Leisure 1
(The Peak District – Dark Peak area) 1:25,000.
See Key to Walks on page 121.

ROUTE DIRECTIONS

From the car park walk
towards **Holmfirth** town
centre. Turn right up Cooper
Lane just before the traffic
lights and walk uphill to the
junction with Holt Lane. Turn
right then immediately left at
a public footpath sign and
take the steep stepped path.
Turn left at the top along a
metalled road between
buildings and then along a
walled lane winding through
open country to the village of
Upperthong. Go straight
ahead through the village,
along Towngate, and at the
end turn left at a junction.

After 50 yards (46m)
downhill, turn right into
another walled lane. Pass the
Newlands Inn and descend,
cross a road and continue
downhill on a minor road.
Before the bridge, turn sharp
left along a lane and descend
through a wooded valley
with a stream on the right. At
Liphill Bank, at the bottom of
the descent, turn sharp right
on the road, go over the
bridge and follow the road
up to Booth House. At the
top of the first steep section
turn left at a post box. The
road winds through the tiny
settlement.

Turn sharp right up a lane
at the back of the Booth

*Make sure you call in at the
Wrinkled Stocking Café in
Holmfirth*

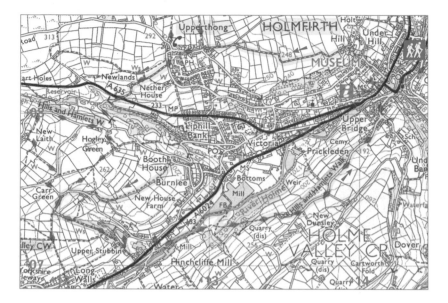

House Gallery, then left along a path beside a wall. Go over a stile then diagonally across a field to a gateway in the far corner. Keep along the left edge of the next four fields, through a gate and down a walled lane to a hamlet. Turn right at the road junction then sharp left just beyond the converted school. After a white gate the lane swings left down a small valley. Above a reservoir cross a metalled drive then turn left between two houses. Cross a field to a white wicket gate then continue to the main road.

Go straight across and bear left along Old Road. Cross a junction and walk along Water Street. Ignore a footbridge at the end of the mill buildings and keep ahead on a path between the **River Holme** and a feeder branch to a reservoir. At the reservoir turn right over a footbridge and take the path to the right, rising to a path crossroads near a wood. Turn left and continue to enter the wood at a stile. Bear left, then take a right fork uphill through old quarry buildings. Cross the broad path running along the wood and ascend to leave the wood at a stile in a wall. Bear left across two fields to a group of houses. Pass the front of the first house and go up a walled lane to a road. Bear left along the road as it contours the valley side before descending to Holmfirth. At a T-junction turn left downhill to the town centre. Cross the road and walk to the bus station with the river on the left. A riverside path leads from the bus station to the car park.

POINTS OF INTEREST

Holmfirth

The television series *Last of the Summer Wine* put Holmfirth on the map. Surprisingly, the café featured in the series is exactly what it seems; a proper old-fashioned café, straight out of the 1950s. A good indicator of its pedigree is the fact that it welcomes cyclists and walkers.

Upperthong

Farming/weaving villages like Upperthong were established long before the town; settlements on the terraces of the valley sprang up during the 15th and 16th centuries, though most of the surviving buildings date back only two or three hundred years. In three-storey cottages families worked at hand looms on the top floor; in older two-storey buildings the bedroom had to double as the loomshop. Daylight to work by was essential and free, hence the rows of windows.

The River Holme

The fast-flowing Holme has cut a narrow gorge through the gritstone hills. Water power brought prosperity to Holmfirth, but it has also brought death when, in 1852, the nearby Bilberry Dam burst and the flood claimed 81 lives.

Historic Langsett now lies beside a reservoir

WHAT IS A NATIONAL PARK?

Britain's National Parks are not national property. Most of the land is privately owned, but the designated area is administered by a National Park Authority. It is their task to strike an appropriate balance between the conservation of the park's characteristic landscape, architecture and wildlife, to ensure that the local population can make a living and to allow access to the millions of visitors who come to appreciate that landscape. The Peak District National Park operates a number of Information Centres, such as the one at Langsett, providing a wide range of publications and organising walks and talks.

LANGSETT   South Yorkshire Map ref SE2100

The northeast corner of the Peak District is probably the least visited sweep of country for 50 miles (80.5km) around; driving south from Holmfirth or west from Penistone takes you across open moors and plateaux with the whole of Yorkshire spread out below in a cerulean haze. There are very few villages to catch your immediate attention, but the upper valleys of the Don and the Porter, which rise on the same watershed as the Derwent on Howden Moor, are full of interest. The Porter has been dammed in several places above Stocksbridge and there are good access points to the reservoirs and riverside and up on to the moors.

Langsett provides the best focal point for an exploration of the Porter and its string of pearls. Before the Sheffield Corporation bought up the valley for water catchment this was farmland, with some of the finest medieval cruck-framed farmhouses and barns in the country. Many of the buildings survive, some still as dwellings but few as working farms.

Langsett Barn, bearing a datestone of 1621, is now the village hall but it is open during the season as a National Park Information Centre, and is well worth a visit both for the information and displays relating to the National Park and to see the solid functional beauty of the post and truss construction of the barn. From the car park it is possible to explore the woods and shoreline of Langsett Reservoir or walk along the dam wall, past the crenellated valve tower (a miniature of a tower at Lancaster Castle), to the old stone-built hamlet of Upper Midhope.

Above Langsett Reservoir, the Brook House Bridge gives access to the ancient trackway of the Cut Gate, a drovers' road from the Derwent to Penistone. The track climbs southwards over Midhope Moor, high uncompromising ground inhabited by mountain hares and short-eared owls, littered with prehistoric flints and overlooked by the burial mound of Pike Lowe.

LONGDENDALE Derbyshire Map ref SK0397

Above Glossop a cleft in the most desolate wilderness of Peak moorland runs north by northeast from the little town of Tintwistle to the Derbyshire-Yorkshire border, shielding the A628 as it climbs to Gallows Moss. Down the cleft runs the River Etherow, a tributary of the Mersey. Over a century ago the valley was dammed to create five reservoirs, and this has so altered the character of the place that it sometimes looks like an oasis in a desert; green woodland and pasture encircles pools of silver, over which white sailing dinghies pirouette and scud.

Longdendale (see Walk on page 106) is a favourite place for day trips out of Manchester, and the cultural roots of Tintwistle are entwined with the Lancashire cotton mills. The waters of the Etherow were harnessed to power the mills and were dammed to provide water for the thirsty city. Railway lines were laid to link the great industrial cities of Manchester and Sheffield, following the valley up to Woodhead and the Prough, a 3-mile (4.8-km) tunnel below the moors. But now all that is in the distant past; the weavers' cottages of Tintwistle are now picturesque and the course of the railway is a footpath. Nevertheless, the dale still serves the city in its own way and remains part of its heritage.

The graveyard of lonely Woodhead Chapel, on a shoulder above the banks of the upper reservoir, contains the last resting place of navvies and their families who died of cholera while the second railway tunnel was being built in 1849. Crowden, above Torside Reservoir, is a famous youth hostel on the route of the Pennine Way and is a welcome sight to walkers after the rigours of Bleaklow to the south or Black Hill to the north. Apart from isolated farms and a National Park Information Centre there are no other settlements in the valley; despite the fine scenery Longdendale often suffers from a wild climate, in the shadow of the moors.

FLOODED FARMLAND
The enclosed fields on the slopes of the valley were probably intended for summering cattle. In the days of open-field farming, crops of corn were grown on the flatter or more fertile ground in the valley bottom, but this, of course, is now under water.

Memorials at lonely Woodhead Chapel recall the harsh lives of the 19th-century tunnel builders

THE SNAKE INN

The Snake Inn was built in 1821 as Lady Clough House, when the original medieval track was transformed into a turnpike road. If any visitor should need a reminder about how remote this hostelry is, there is a stone outside which records 21 miles to Manchester, 17 to Sheffield.

The remote Snake Pass Inn is liable to find itself cut off from the rest of the world in wintertime

THE SNAKE PASS Derbyshire

Weather warnings on television and radio have made The Snake Pass famous; when the sun is shining across the rest of the Pennines, The Snake Pass, the A57 between Sheffield and Manchester, may be closed because of severe blizzards.

The road from Ladybower and the Woodlands Valley strikes northwest, sheltered on a shoulder of the River Ashop, but after Lady Clough it has nowhere to hide and crosses a windswept desert at 1,680 feet (512m). Bleaklow lies to the north, Kinder Scout to the south. In places the peat has been stripped away to reveal a surface of shattered stones, which is how the glaciers left the place after the Ice Age. There are no trees, no barns or walls. Not a good place to be stuck in a car.

Of course, the remote wildness of The Snake is irresistible and in fine weather, with the sun shining on the heather, it can be magical. The upper Woodlands Valley is pretty, dotted with old farms and birch-lined cloughs. Most of the Peak District has been designated as an Environmentally Sensitive Area, which means farmers get special payments for agreeing to manage the land with conservation in mind. In the case of the high moors, the most important thing is the stocking rate – fewer sheep are now overwintered on the heather, and this should benefit the flora and fauna.

A tributary of the Ashop runs north to Alport Dale and Alport Castle, which is not a castle at all, but an outcrop of rock; this is accessible by a bridleway and makes a good walk. The barn of Alport Castle Farm is used on the first Sunday in July each year for a Lovefeast service. These 'love feasts' originated during the 18th-century religious revival that was spearheaded by the Wesley brothers. They converted multitudes of workers, from

mines and mills, farms and factories, to a pattern of religious life which inspired them to build 'wayside Bethels' in remote places. Along with field preaching, their ministers organised camp-meetings and covenant services, incorporating 'love feasts' which were based on the meetings of the early Church.

Back along the Snake Road there are two or three last farms and cottages before the lonely Snake Pass Inn is reached. At the top of Lady Clough, on the highest and most featureless ground, The Snake is crossed by the Pennine Way, close to the paved trackway of ancient Doctor's Gate. Travellers have been venturing across these moors for thousands of years, often with a shiver of apprehension.

A milestone at the inn records the distance to civilisation

SNAKE BY NAME...
While driving across the high moorland on the Snake Pass it is easy to suppose that it derived its name from the serpent-like twists and turns of the road. Not so. The snake comes from a device on the crest of the Cavendish family, the Dukes of Devonshire.

The Dark Peak

Leisure Information

Places of Interest

Shopping

Sports, Activities

and the Outdoors

Annual Events and Customs

✓ Checklist

Leisure Information

TOURIST INFORMATION CENTRES

Glossop
The Gatehouse, Victoria Street.
Tel: 01457 855920.
Holmfirth
49–51 Huddersfield Road.
Tel: 01484 222444.
Saddleworth
High Street, Uppermill, Oldham.
Tel: 01457 874093.

NATIONAL PARK CENTRES

Head Office
Baslow Road, Bakewell.
Tel: 01629 816200.
www.peakdistrict.org.uk
Castleton
Castle Street. Tel: 01433
620679.
Edale
Fieldhead (right of road from
Edale Station to village).
Tel: 01433 670207.
Fairholmes (Derwent Valley)
Tel: 01433 650953.

OTHER INFORMATION

Derbyshire Wildlife Trust
Elvaston Castle, Derby.
Tel: 01332 756610.
English Nature
Manor Barn, Over Haddon,
Bakewell. Tel: 01629 815095.

Forestry Commission
Sherwood and Lincs Forest
District, Edwinstowe, Mansfield.
Tel: 01623 822447.
National Trust
Regional Office: Clumber Park
Stableyard, Worksop, Notts.
Tel: 01909 486411.
High Peak and Longshaw Estate
Office: Tel: 01433 670368.
www.nationaltrust.org.uk
North West Water
Dawson House, Great Sankey,
Warrington. Tel: 01925 234000.
Public Transport
The 'Derbyshire Wayfarer' allows
one day's unlimited travel on
local buses and trains in the
county. Details from Derbyshire
County Council, Public
Transport Dept. Tel: 01629
580000.
Derbyshire Busline Tel: 01298
23098.
GMPTE Tel: 0161 288 7811.
South Yorkshire Travelline Tel:
01709 515151.
Rail information Tel: 0345
484950.
www.derbysbus.net
Severn Trent Water
2297 Coventry Road,
Birmingham. Tel: 0121 722
4968.
Staffordshire Wildlife Trust
Coutts House, Sandon, Stafford.
Tel: 01889 508534.

Weather Call
Tel: 0906 850 0417.
Yorkshire Water
2 The Embankment, Sovereign
Street, Leeds. Tel: 0113 234
3234.

ORDNANCE SURVEY MAPS

Landranger 1:50,000 Sheet 110.
Outdoor Leisure 1:25,000
Sheet 1

Places of Interest

There will be an admission
charge at the following places of
interest unless otherwise stated.
Glossop Heritage Centre
Henry Street, Glossop. Tel:
01457 869176. Open all year,
daily. Free.
Peak Cavern
on A625, Castleton.
Tel: 01433 620285. Open
Easter–Oct, daily; Nov–Easter
weekends.
Peveril Castle
Castleton. Tel: 01433 620613.
Open all year, most days.
Speedwell Cavern
off A625, ½ mile (0.8km) west of
Castleton. Tel: 01433 620512.
Open all year, daily except
Christmas Day.
Treak Cliff Cavern
Three quarters of a mile (1.2km)
west of Castleton on the

A625.Tel: 01433 620571. Open all year, daily except 25 Dec.

Shopping

Glossop
Indoor market Thu; indoor and outdoor market Fri and Sat.
Holmfirth
Craft market, Sat and Bank Hols. General market Thu.

LOCAL SPECIALITIES

Blue John Jewellery
Speedwell Caverns Ltd, Winnats Pass, Castleton. Tel: 01433 620512.
Also available from other local outlets.
Craft workshops
Glossop Craft Centre, No 1 Smithy Fold, off High Street East, Glossop. Tel: 01457 863559.

Sports, Activities and the Outdoors

CAVING

Edale
YHA Activity Centre, Rowland Cote, Nether Booth. Tel: 01433 670302.
Hathersage
Rock Lea Activity Centre, Station Road. Tel: 01433 650345.

COUNTRY PARK

Etherow Country Park, George Street, Compsall, Stockport. Tel: 0161 4276937.

CYCLING

The Sett Valley Trail
This trail runs for 2½ miles (4km) from New Mills to Hayfield.

CYCLE HIRE

Hope
Hope Cycle Hire, Unit 2, Castleton Road. Tel: 01433 623113.
Hayfield
Derbyshire Countryside Information Service. Tel: 01663 746222.

GOLF COURSES

Glossop
Glossop Golf Club, Sheffield Road.
Tel: 01457 853117.

New Mills
New Mills, Shaw Marsh. Tel: 01663 743485.

GUIDED WALKS

Castleton
The walks, for which a charge is made, last approximately 1½ hours. They start from the Castleton Visitor Centre, Jun–Sep.
For details contact the Castleton Visitor Centre.
Glossop
The walks, for which a charge is made, last approximately 1½ hours. They start from Glossop Tourist Information Centre. For details contact Glossop Tourist Information Centre.
Longdendale
Contact Tourist Information Centre.
National Park Walks with a Ranger
Contact Peak District National Park 24-hour information line Tel: 01629 816327.

HORSE-RIDING

Charlesworth
Harqate Hill Equestrian Centre, Glossop Road. Tel: 01457 865518.
Edale
Lady Booth Riding Centre. Tel: 01433 670205.

LONG-DISTANCE FOOTPATHS AND TRAILS

The Limestone Way
Runs for 26 miles (41.8km) from Matlock to Castleton.
The Pennine Way.
Runs for 256 miles (412km) from Edale to Kirk Yetholm, just over the border in Scotland.
The Sett Valley Trail
This trail runs for 2½ miles (4km), from New Mills to Hayfield.

ROCK-CLIMBING

Edale
Edale YHA Activity Centre, Rowland Cote, Nether Booth. Tel: 01433 670302.
Hathersage
Rock Lea Activity Centre, Peak Activities Ltd, Station Road. Tel: 01433 650345.

Pennine Way stile at Edale

WATERSPORTS

Hathersage
Rock Lea Activity Centre, Peak Activities Ltd, Station Road. Tel: 01433 650345. Also helicopter rides.

Annual Events and Customs

Alport Castle
Alport Love Feast in Alport Barn. Access via Heyridge Farm on A57, early July.
Castleton
Garland Ceremony, late June.
Edale
Bluegrass Music Festival, early June
Glossop
Jazz Festival, mid-June. Carnival and Country Fair, early July. Victorian weekend, early September. Well-dressing, mid- to late September.
Hayfield
Sheepdog Trials, late September
Holmfirth
Folk Festival, early May.
Hope
Well-dressing late June–early July. Sheepdog Trials and Agricultural Show, late August.

The checklists give details of just some of the facilities within the area covered by this guide. Further information is available from Tourist Information Centres.

Atlas and Map Symbols

THE NATIONAL GRID SYSTEM

The National Grid system covers Great Britain with an imaginary network of 100 kilometre grid squares. Each square is given a unique alphabetic reference as shown in the diagram. These squares are sub-divided into one hundred 10 kilometre squares, each numbered from 0 to 9 in an easterly (left to right) direction and northerly (upwards) direction from the bottom left corner. Each 10 km square is similarly sub-divided into one hundred 1 km squares.

Kilometres North

						HP	
					HT	HU	
					HY	HZ	
NA	NB	NC	ND				
NF	NG	NH	NJ	NK			
NL	NM	NN	NO				
	NR	NS	NT	NU			
	NW	NX	NY	NZ			
		SC	SD	SE	TA		
		SH	SJ	SK	TF	TG	
	SM	SN	SO	SP	TL	TM	
	SR	SS	ST	SU	TQ	TR	
SV	SW	SX	SY	SZ	TV		

False Origin of National Grid   Kilometres East

KEY TO ATLAS

⌘	Abbey, cathedral or priory	– – – – –	National trail
◄	Aquarium	NT	National Trust property
♜	Castle	NTS	National Trust for Scotland property
⌒	Cave	⬥	Nature reserve
♈	Country park	★	Other place of interest
⛾	County cricket ground	P·R	Park and Ride location
⛺	Farm or animal centre	♣	Picnic site
·········	Forest drive	🚂	Steam centre
❄	Garden	⛷	Ski slope natural
⛳	Golf course	⛷	Ski slope artifical
🏛	Historic house	🄸	Tourist Information Centre
🐎	Horse racing	☀	Viewpoint
🏁	Motor racing	☑	Visitor or heritage centre
🏛	Museum	🦌	Zoological or wildlife collection
☎	AA telephone		Forest Park
⊕	Airport		Heritage coast
Ⓗ	Heliport		National Park (England & Wales)
🌾	Windmill		National Scenic Area (Scotland)

KEY TO ATLAS

MOTORWAY		A ROAD	
═M4═	Motorway with number	A1123	Other A road single/dual carriageway
═S═ Fleet	Motorway service area	═════	Road tunnel
═①═	Motorway junction with and without number	─Toll─	Toll
═③═	Restricted motorway junctions	▬▬▬▬	Road under construction
═══	Motorway and junction under construction	✛	Roundabout
PRIMARY ROUTE		**B ROAD**	
═A3═	Primary route single/dual carriageway	B2070	B road single/dual carriageway
═S═ Grantham North	Primary route service area	✛	B road interchange junction
BATH	Primary route destinations	✛	B road roundabout with adjoining unclassified road
✛	Roundabout	──>	Steep gradient
▼ 5 ▼	Distance in miles between symbols	───	Unclassified road single/dual carriageway
▬▬▬	Narrow Primary route with passing places	─o─×─	Railway station and level crossing

KEY TO TOURS

🚗	Tour start point	Buckland Abbey	Highlighted point of interest
➡	Direction of tour		
▶▶·▶▶	Optional detour	▬▬▬	Featured tour

KEY TO WALKS

Scale 1:25,000, 2½ inches to 1 mile, 4cm to 1 km

🚶	Start of walk		Line of walk
➤	Direction of walk	⊪➤⊪	Optional detour
		Buckland Abbey	Highlighted point of interest

ROADS AND PATHS

M1 or A6(M)	M1 or A6(M)	Motorway
A 31(T) or A35	A 31(T) or A35	Trunk or main road
B 3074	B 3074	Secondary road
A 35	A 35	Dual carriageway
		Road generally more than 4m wide
		Road generally less than 4m wide
		Other road, drive or track
		Path

Unfenced roads and tracks are shown by pecked lines

RAILWAYS

Multiple track	Standard gauge		Embankment
Single track			Tunnel
	Narrow gauge		Road over; road under
	Siding		Level crossing
	Cutting		Station

PUBLIC RIGHTS OF WAY

Public rights of way may not be evident on the ground

	Public paths { footpath / bridleway	+ +	Byway open to all traffic
	Permissive path		Road used as a public path
	Permissive bridleway	◆ ◆	Named path
		Pennine Way	National trail or recreational path

The representation on this map of any other road, track or path is no evidence of the existence of a right of way

RELIEF

50 ·	Heights determined by	Ground survey
285 ·		Air survey

Contours are at 5 and 10 metres vertical interval

SYMBOLS

Place of worship { with tower / with spire, minaret or dome / without such additions	○W, Spr	Well, Spring
		Gravel pit
Building		Other pit or quarry
Important building		Sand pit
Telephone: public; AA; RAC	. T; A; R	Refuse or slag heap
Electricity transmission line	pylon pole	County Boundary (England & Wales)
Triangulation pillar	△ △	
Bus or coach station		Water
Lighthouse; beacon		Sand; sand & shingle
Site of antiquity		National Park boundary
National Trust always open	NT	
Forestry Commission	FC	Mud

DANGER AREA

Firing and test ranges in the area
Danger!
Observe warning notices

VEGETATION

Limits of vegetation are defined by positioning of the symbols but may be delineated also by pecks or dots

🌲	Coniferous trees	○	Non-coniferous trees
	Orchard		Heath
	Coppice		Marsh, reeds, saltings.

TOURIST AND LEISURE INFORMATION

Δ	Camp site	PC	Public convenience
🛈	Information centre	P	Parking
i	Information centre (seasonal)	🔆	Viewpoint
🚐	Caravan site	⊕	Mountain rescue post
✕	Picnic site		

Index

A

Alport Castle 116, 119
Ambergate 82
Aquarium and Hologram Gallery, Matlock Bath 99
Arbor Low Stone Circle 9, 66, 68
Ashbourne 12, 28, 29
Ashford in the Water 49, 69
Axe Edge 35, 42

B

Back Forest 42, 44
Bakewell 52, 69
Bakewell Circular Walk 69
Bamford 99
Baslow 8, 70, 72, 99
Beeley 77, 78, 79
Beresford Dale 10, 18, 19
Biggin Dale 10
Blackbrook – The Zoological Park of the Moorlands, Leek 47
Black Rock, Wirksworth 25
Blackshaw Moor 35
Blue John 101
Bottoms Reservoir 107
Bradwell 111
Brassington 15
Brindley Mill, Leek 46
Brindley Trail 48
Buxton 11, 30, 34, 46, 47, 48

C

Caldon Canal 38
Calver 72, 73, 74
Carsington Water 14, 29
Castle Hill, Glossop 105
Castleton 11, 100, 119
Cat and Fiddle Inn, Goyt Valley 33
Cat and Fiddle Moor 33
Caudwell Mill, Rowsley 85, 98
Cave Dale, Castleton 102
Chapel-en-le-Frith 11, 32, 34, 46, 73
Chatsworth 8, 75, 78, 98, 99
Chatsworth Farm & Adventure Playground 99
Chatsworth Farm Shop, Pilsley 77
Cheddleton 38, 48
Cheddleton Flint Mill 38, 46
Cheddleton Railway Centre 38, 47
Chesterfield 80, 98, 99
Chestnut Centre, Chapel-en-le-Frith 46
Churchtown 84, 85
Coombes Valley 35
Cratcliffe Rocks, Youlgreave 67
Cressbrook Dale 57, 59, 64
Cressbrook Mill 59
Crich 81, 99
Cromford 82, 99
Cromford Canal 82
Cromford Mill 83, 98
Curbar 74
Cut Gate 114
Cut-thorn Hill 42

D

Darley Bridge 87
Darley Dale 84, 87
Derwent Crystal, Ashbourne 27

Derwent Dams 11, 88
Derwent Reservoir 88
Derwent Valley 82
Dovedale 10, 18, 29
Dove Holes 11, 34

E

Eagle Stone, Baslow 70
Ecton Copper Mines 16
Edale 103, 119
Edensor 77
Errwood Reservoir, Goyt Valley 33, 36
Etherow Country Park, Compsall 119
Eyam 53, 69, 73
Eyam Hall 68
Eyam Museum 68

F

Fawfieldhead 21
Fenny Bentley 25
Fernilee 34
Fernilee Reservoir, Goyt Valley 33
Flash 35, 42
Forest Visitor Centre, near Macclesfield 41
Froggatt Edge 90, 95

G

Gawsworth Hall 41
Glossop 11, 73, 104, 119
Goyt Moss 33, 37
Goyt Valley 33, 36
Gradbach 42, 44
Gradbach Mill 44
Grindleford 72, 89, 99
Grindsbrook Booth, Edale 103
Grinlow & Buxton Country Park 47
Gritstone Trail 41, 48
Gulliver's Kingdom, Matlock Bath 93, 99

H

Haddon Hall 54, 68
Hare Hill 47
Hartington 9, 10, 19, 29
Hathersage 72, 91, 99, 119
Hayfield 73, 108, 119
Heights of Abraham, Matlock Bath 92, 93, 98
Heritage Centre, Glossop 104, 118
Heritage Centre, Macclesfield 40
High Peak Junction Workshops, Wirksworth 27, 83
High Peak Trail 15, 25, 29, 83
Holmfirth 109, 112, 113, 119
Hope 110, 119
Hope Cross 97
Hope Valley 102
Hopton 15
Howden Reservoir 88
Hunting Tower, Chatsworth 79

I/K

Ilam 10, 20, 29
Ilam Park 20, 27
Kinder Scout 103, 108
King's Chair 15

L

Ladybower Reservoir 72, 88, 96, 97
Langsett 114
Langsett Barn 114
Langsett Reservoir 114
Lathkill Dale 55, 69
Lea Gardens, Matlock 98
Leek 35, 38, 47, 48
Limestone Way 67, 99, 119
Litton 9, 58, 59, 64, 69
Longdendale 115, 119
Longdendale Trail 106
Longnor 11, 21, 29, 35
Longnor Craft Centre 27
Longshaw Estate 90
Longshaw Lodge Visitor Centre 94
Lud's Church 45
Lyme Park 39, 41, 47

M

Macclesfield 40, 47, 48
Magpie Mine, Sheldon 51
Mam Tor, Castleton 101
Manifold Trail 17, 23, 29
Manifold Valley 10, 22
Market House, Winster 65, 68
Mass Trespass, Hayfield 108
Matlock 92, 99
Matlock Bath 92, 99
Melandra Castle, Glossop 105
Middleton by Wirksworth 26
Middleton by Youlgreave 69
Middleton Dale 73
Middleton Top Engine House, Middleton by Wirksworth 27
Middlewood Way 48
Midhope Moor 114
Mill Dale 10, 18
Miller's Dale 9, 56, 57, 59, 64
Monks Dale 57
Monsal Trail 48, 56, 69
Monyash 55, 69
Museum & Art Gallery, Buxton 46
Museum & Art Gallery, Chesterfield 98

N

National Stone Centre, Wirksworth 25, 28
National Tramway Museum, Crich 81, 98
Nether End 71
Nether Padley 72, 89
Newbold Moor 80
Nine Ladies Stone Circle 62, 98
Nine Rings Stone Circle, Youlgreave 67

O

Oker Hill 87
Old House Museum, Bakewell 52, 68
Old Whittington 80, 99
Over Haddon 55

P/Q

Padley 11
Padley Gorge 89, 94, 95

Padley Hall 89
Paradise Mill, Macclesfield 47
Parsley Hay 9
Pavilion Gardens, Buxton 31, 47
Peacock Information and Heritage
   Centre, Chesterfield 98
Peak Cavern, Castleton 101, 118
Peak District Mining Museum,
   Matlock 92, 98
Peak Forest 60
Peak Rail, Matlock 98
Pennine Way 103, 109, 117,
   119
Peveril Castle, Castleton 102,
   118
Pike Lowe 114
Pilsbury Castle 19
Pilsley 69, 77
Poole's Cavern, Buxton 47
Pym Chair 37
Queen Mary's Bower, Chatsworth
   79

R

Ramshaw Rocks 35, 42
Ravenstor 58
Revolution House, Old Whittington
   80, 99
Roaches, The 42, 44
Robin Hood's Stride, Youlgreave
   67
Rowsley 85, 99
Rowtor Rocks, Youlgreave 62, 67
Rushton Spencer 41

S

St Ann's Well, Buxton 30
Sett Valley Trail 73, 108, 119
Seven Wonders of the Peak 64
Shining Tor 33, 36
Silk Museum, Macclesfield 47
Snake Inn, Snake Pass 72, 116
Snake Pass 11, 116

Spanish Shrine 36
Speedwell Cavern, Castleton 101,
   118
Staffordshire Way 48
Stanton in Peak 61
Steeple Grange Light Railway,
   Middleton by Wirksworth 28
Stoney Middleton 69, 73, 99
Sugarloaf 16
Sunday School, Macclesfield 40
Sutton Lane Ends 41
Swainsley Tunnel 17
Swine Sty 90

T

Taxal 43
Tegg's Nose Country Park 41
Temple Mine, Matlock 92, 99
Thorpe Cloud 22
Thor's Cave 17, 23
Three Shires Head 42
Tideswell 9, 58, 63, 69, 73
Tideswell Dale 58, 64
Tin Town 88
Tintwistle 106, 115
Tintwistle Low Moor 106
Tissington 23, 24, 29
Tissington Trail 19, 24, 29
Tittesworth Reservoir 39, 47
Treak Cliff Cavern, Castleton
   101, 119

U

Upper Booth, Edale 103
Upper Hulme 35
Upper Midhope 114
Upper Padley 89
Upperthong 113

W/Y

Warren, The, Chatsworth 79
Warslow 10, 22, 35
Water-cum-Jolly Dale 59

Waterhouses 23
Wellington Monument, Baslow
   Edge 70
Wensley 87
Wensley Dale 87
West Park Museum, Macclesfield
   47
Wetton 16, 22
Wetton Hill 22
Wettonmill 17
Whaley Bridge 34, 43
Whatstandwell 82
Whistlestop Countryside Centre,
   Matlock Bath 99
Wildboarclough 43
Win Hill 97, 110
Wincle Minn 44
Winnats Pass 101
Winster 65, 68, 69
Wirksworth 25, 28, 29
Wirksworth Heritage Centre 28
Wolfscote Dale 10, 18
Woodlands Valley 11, 72, 88,
   116
Working Carriage Museum, Darley
   Dale 99
Wormhill 38, 57, 69
Wye Valley 61
Youlgreave 9, 66, 69

Chatsworth and the
Emperor Fountain, a
290-feet (88m) jet of water

Acknowledgements

The Automobile Association wishes to thank the following photographers and libraries for their assistance in the preparation of this book.

THE MANSELL COLLECTION 6d
NATURE PHOTOGRAPHERS LTD 7e (P R Sterry)

All remaining pictures are held in the Association's own library (AA PHOTO LIBRARY) and were taken by A J HOPKINS with the exception page 127 which was taken by P BAKER, pages 39, 40, 61, 111 were taken by M BIRKITT, page 6b was taken by R NEWTON and page 55 by A TRYNOR.